S0-BOC-308

PHOTO: DARRELL HENRY

Peter Huyck was born in Des Moines, Iowa, in 1940 and has a B.A. in philosophy from the University of Iowa. He served in the U.S. Air Force for four years and worked as a programmer for IBM's Programming Advanced Technology group and for Westinghouse Learning Corporation before taking up writing full time. He lives in Iowa City.

Nellie Kremenak was born in Des Moines, Iowa, in 1934. She has a B.A. in history and an M.A. in library science, both from the University of Iowa. She works as an information specialist at the Dows Institute for Dental Research at the University of Iowa, and lives in Iowa City.

DESIGN & MEMORY

DESIGN & MEMORY

COMPUTER PROGRAMMING IN THE 20TH CENTURY

PETER H. HUYCK
and
NELLIE W. KREMENAK

McGRAW-HILL BOOK COMPANY
New York St. Louis San Francisco Sydney Paris Hamburg Auckland Bogotá São Paulo London New Delhi Mexico Tokyo Johannesburg Panama Singapore Montreal Madrid

For Lucian J. Endicott, Jr.

Library of Congress Cataloging in Publication Data

Huyck, Peter H
Design & memory.

Includes bibliographical references and index.
1. Electronic digital computers—Programming.
I. Kremenak, Nellie W., joint author. II. Title.
QA76.6.H89 001.64'2 80-11108
ISBN 0-07-031554-X

1 2 3 4 5 6 7 8 9 0 MUMU 8 9 8 7 6 5 4 3 2 1 0

The editors for this book were Barry Richman and Carolyn B. Nagy, the designer was Elliot Epstein, and the production supervisor was Teresa F. Leaden. It was set in Palatino by Bi-Comp, Incorporated.

Printed and bound by The Murray Printing Company.

CONTENTS

PREFACE

There is a tendency among computer programmers to take the logic of the machine at face value. Problems for which there are no algorithmic solutions are perceived as unreal or imperfectly understood. This outlook necessarily limits the usefulness of computers.

Programmers also have a tendency to think that human history began in about 1950. In fact, the two main components of computing—design and memory—have been with us a long time. History will teach us a lot if we just listen.

This book is an attempt—albeit slightly irreverent—to look at where the programming phenomenon came from, what it is, and where it is going. We suggest some new ways of looking at digital computing and, in addition, provide a little consciousness-raising for the programming profession.

We want to acknowledge our intellectual debt to Hugh Kenner, Buckminster Fuller, Stephen Toulmin, Ronald Stamper, and Hubert Dreyfus. They may prefer not to claim us, but nevertheless, their work has had considerable influence on our thinking.

Peter H. Huyck

Nellie W. Kremenak

ONE

BOOTSTRAPPING OUR WAY IN

THE UBIQUITOUS VANISHING PROGRAMMER

Frequently, one reads in the trade press one or the other of the following contradictory views (in fact, both views occasionally appear in a single issue):

1. Soon, everyone will be a programmer. The need for programmers is increasing at an exponential rate, and in the future business people, homemakers, and communards will all be writing code.
2. Soon, no one will be a programmer. Programmers will be reduced to the status of minor clerks. Programmers are expensive prima donnas who only create problems and must be dispensed with.

When one finds contradictory views such as these being frequently and honestly espoused, one turns to dialectics in an attempt to determine what is in fact the case. When we examine the arguments of the opposing camps, we find that they arise from a single assumption, namely, that things cannot possibly go on as they are. The conclusion one draws from this assumption—that things will either get worse or go away—tends to depend on how one feels about programmers.

The view that things cannot remain the same is correct. The subview that everyone will be a programmer is obviously false if it is taken to mean that people in all walks of life will be writing BASIC, but certainly access to large computers through home terminals and the proliferation of microprocessors will make the technology available to practically everyone. The subview that no one will be programming is obviously true if it is taken to mean that the big COBOL shops will die slowly on the vine.

Someone will be doing real programming, however, and it is likely that more rather than fewer people will be involved. They will be programming with very different tools. They will not be minor clerks but information impresarios, probably forming an identifiable profession with many specialties, probably still highly paid and much in demand. Certainly they will have a larger repertory of information skills than we commonly associate with programmers today. In point of fact, the more successful programming teams already draw on a broad base of information skills. They have had to solve the problems of documentation, continuity, testing, and maintenance—the very problems that those programmers who are said to be either proliferating or becoming extinct or both have failed to solve.

It has been observed that this country is run by people in their forties. Large numbers of programmers are just beginning to turn 40. What influence are they likely to have on the running of the world? Very few businesses, government agencies, or universities as yet have programmers in the highest reaches of their decision-making apparatus, yet most of these institutions would have great difficulty functioning without their data processing departments. It is still an open question whether programmers will share in the running of the world, but clearly there can be no doubt that at the minimum our profession—or discipline or science or craft or art or whatever it is—will have a great influence.

Brash young programmers have always been a problem. It is probable that programmers mellow somewhat in their middle years. But wait for the old programmers! That is when programming will really begin to come into its own, for programming is an old person's game. Large numbers of programmers will not spill out into marketing and production, as is sometimes predicted, because programming is more fun. They will hang right in there and program.

READING THIS BOOK

As you read this book, do not expect to find "action items." We intend to discuss problems to which there may be no clear-cut solutions. We are hovering in search of the right questions. Listen to Albert Szent-Györgyi: "Science is built on the experience that Nature answers intelligent questions intelligently; thus if Nature is silent, something may be wrong with the question."[1] We expect the answers to the questions raised in these pages, as well as ever-more-refined formulations of the questions themselves, to arise from the aspect of Nature we call "programming." The exercises for students are for exercise.

WHAT THIS BOOK IS ABOUT

This book is about programmers, programming, and programs. We are going to try to assess our present professional difficulties and suggest some ways out of them. In the short history of programming, where has the formulation of the proper questions been undertaken? Programming to date has ridden piggyback on the goals and problems of other enterprises and has thereby failed to emerge as a professional discipline in its own right.

Our basic approach is to overreach. Many scientific innovators were seen in their time as interlopers, if not outright poachers. Physics, for example, was frequently thought to be poaching on theology's ground, as indeed biology is still doing to some degree today. In fact (no use hiding it), we too intend to poach on sacred ground.

Information is tied to language and language informs behavior, so one must proceed very carefully. Tampering with language is as fraught with peril as is tampering with genes. To zero in on the principles of information is to come very near the heart of the matter.

The contention that a continuous, infinite process can be hosted in discrete, finite components is apt to get a friendly hearing from those who hold that God is eternal and humanity His temporal embodiment. However, to recognize a silicon chip as His newest embodiment may be difficult for some. When we contend further that the laws of Nature allow local shaping of the continuum through human intervention, only the most advanced theologians are likely to receive gracefully the correlative idea that humanity changes the face of God. (Of course, humanity is continually changing the face of God, as anthropologists are aware. How God may feel about this is another matter.)

PROGRAMMING

In his book on Buckminster Fuller, *Bucky: A Guided Tour of Buckminster Fuller* (New York, William Morrow, 1973, p. 7), Hugh Kenner points out that "we get our everyday language . . . from . . . the visible environment," especially from what we perceive to be successful and lasting human gestures.* Thus we frequently speak about programming by such unspecified analogies, especially intuitive analogies to architecture. These metaphors arise naturally from what we see around us, much of which is now of our own creation. Programming, however, is not visible in the environment, and it doesn't tend to last. This suggests that we

* Reading Kenner's book, we sometimes find it difficult to disentangle Kenner's thinking from Fuller's. We will compound the problem by making it difficult to disentangle our thinking from theirs, thus expressing our debt to both.

have misunderstood some themes: certainly misreading either architecture or programming and perhaps misreading the human effort as well. Fuller speaks of whole systems. Reality flows, but it flows through persistent knottings so that one need feel no vertigo. Solids are the fraternity of the fallen-in-together.[2] What, then, are programs?

Our profession has had difficulty finding the right words to explain what we are doing, so we attempt to explain it with inappropriate words and then come to believe our own inadequate explanations. For example, it is often said that a program is like a recipe. How unlike a recipe is a program! Thirty minutes spent reading *The Joy of Cooking* should be enough to convince us that a program is not like a recipe. One could make an excellent case for saying that programs should be like recipes, but to say that they are is nonsense.

When we talk about computer programming, what are we really talking about? Machines, instructions, data, information, algorithms: What does this whole parcel amount to? What is this phenomenon in the history of humankind?

Everything functions as the context of everything else. This involves a difficulty because it seems to leave no secure reference points.[3] But consider the great monuments at Stonehenge. There is a good example of an ambitious project sustained over time in a world of flux. They spent more time moving in one block of stone than we spend building an entire operating system, and they didn't have any better idea of what life is all about than we do. (If they had discovered the point of life, you can bet we'd have heard about it; they lived only about 150 generations ago.) As with stone, so with digital storage. We believe that an ambitious project can be sustained in digital storage.

EXERCISE FOR STUDENTS

Every programmer should go to Stonehenge. Go.

ADVANCED EXERCISE

See if you can get your manager to pay for the trip.

Long ago, rock was first differentiated out of the earth; much later, metal was differentiated out of the rock.[4] Eventually electricity was differentiated out of the metal, and now, in our own time, digital storage is being differentiated out of the electricity. Let us recognize that this is the tradition in which we stand, that working with digital storage is in fact similar to working with stone, and that many of the techniques are the same and have, in fact, descended directly to us from our ancestors. Equally important is the fact that despite the external changes, the human condition is pretty much the same now as it always has been, and that like our ancestors, we set goals for ourselves and try to reach them with some measure of dignity.

EXERCISE FOR STUDENTS

Describe the human condition (in 25 words or less).

The imminent breakthrough that everyone anticipates in computer programming is analogous to the prehistoric transition from flaking stone to grinding stone. That earlier breakthrough coincided with the transition from hunting to farming. It is likely that the coming breakthrough in computer programming will have equally profound implications, perhaps coinciding with outmigration from the earth.

What links us to those ancient workers in stone? They are all dead now, and we are all alive. What links us is the same thing which will connect us to our descendants 150 generations hence, whatever they are doing. We will all be dead, they will all be alive, and it is the culture that connects us. We communicate with our ancestors and descendants through the culture we all hold in common.

Children react to the new every day, bootstrapping their way into the world with the little they do know, proving that an ambitious project can be sustained in a world of flux. That is how we must enter the world of the massive digital storage resources that the engineers are cooking up. Digital storage is not a large electronic filing cabinet. It is an electric grandmother; a machine in which we can store up and from which we can recall everything we have been, are, and hope to be; a machine which embodies its creators—us—and our aspirations and which at our request can move ahead and explore the paths we wish to take. By the way we build and shape her, we will build and shape ourselves.*

INVISIBLEWARE

Software makes information from data. Information cannot be discussed independently of language or without language, and language is, in fact, often regarded as *the* programming problem. There is a belief, based on a remark of Bertrand Russell's, which states that if we get the language right, the software problems will solve themselves. Getting the language right means bringing it usefully into consonance with the principles of information. This means the programming languages themselves and also the plain old language we use to talk about programs. We do expect that having once grasped the principles of information—if not what it is, at least how it works—we will be able to embody those principles in languages which will in turn be vehicles for a solution to the problems of software.

* This metaphor is borrowed from Ray Bradbury's memorable story "I Sing the Body Electric" in *I Sing the Body Electric*, New York, Knopf, 1969, pp. 150–190.

EXERCISE FOR STUDENTS

Using pseudocode for a pseudomachine, write an "anyrithm" (algorithms are a subset of anyrithms) which will assess a paragraph of text for verisimilitude or determine whether a joke is funny.

(To work this exercise, you need to know the difference between pseudocode and a pseudomachine. "Pseudocode" is a programming language that a programmer makes up for convenience to solve problems. Although there is no compiler for a pseudocode language, it is in principle translatable into an existing language for which there is a compiler. A "pseudomachine" is an architecture that a programmer makes up for convenience to solve problems on, but we relax the condition that the architecture be in principle translatable into an existing architecture. This allows us to write anyrithms which lead the state of the engineering arts. You may assume "wet" engineering; that is, you may use functions which you know perfectly well cannot be digitized.)

MEASURING UP

As a point of departure we will take the work of Stephen Toulmin, as set forth in *Human Understanding* (Princeton, Princeton University Press, 1972). This work adapts Darwin's theory of the evolution of biological species to more general populations. Toulmin has abstracted the notions of variation and selection and elevated them to the status of historiographical principles, applying them to populations of concepts, institutions, and traditions. Toulmin's analysis of the history and philosophy of science is by no means universally accepted, and it finds strong resistance in some quarters. We believe, however, that his analysis is useful and that an examination of his ideas and their relevance to programming will provide new perspectives.

Toulmin discusses the evolution of a particular science from its diffuse origins to the achievement of "proper disciplinary status." Such status is achieved when the practitioners of the discipline agree on a "set of fundamental concepts and selection criteria."[5] For the sake of argument we shall suppose that there exists something called "information science." (For the sake of argument is possibly the only reason one might suppose this.) Information science, then, is related to programming as physics is related to engineering. In Toulmin's terms, programming has at least the potential to be a "collective discipline." Let us measure programming against his standards for a collective discipline.

For Toulmin, the paradigm of a collective discipline can be broken down into several constituent parts:

1. Generally agreed on disciplinary *goals,* which are:
   a. Isolable, and
   b. Held to be of positive value
2. A changing population of recipes and designs, techniques, and manufacturing processes, i.e., a *methodology*
3. A *professional forum* in which to critically examine current procedures and proposed innovations

Goals. Are there agreed-on professional programming goals that can be effectively pursued in isolation from other goals? We think not. The tendency has been toward association with and domination by the goals of big business and big government.

Let us say for the sake of argument that the goal of doctoring is better health for everyone. What is the analogous goal for programming? Gerald Weinberg (*The Psychology of Computer Programming,* New York, D. Van Nostrand, 1971) might say that the goal is to write better programs, but this begs the question. Of course we want to write better programs, but what are we trying to do by writing programs in the first place? Don't assume that someone else is thinking about such matters and that your job is just to code. There isn't anyone here on earth except the 4 billion or so of us who are currently alive. No one is in charge except us. Isn't it likely that figuring out what we are doing will help us do it better? Could our goal be better information for everyone?

EXERCISE FOR STUDENTS

We have some code which allows the banks to know more about us, but where is the code which allows us to know more about the banks? Write this code.

But even that description—better information for everyone—requires some qualification. Toulmin points out that in conceding disciplinary status to an enterprise, we take the positive value of that enterprise for granted. Thus, a discipline whose agreed-on goal was the most effective elimination of large populations by means of a neutron bomb would find its positive value in difficulty with some of us. Can programming's goals claim a presumed positive value? What about Equity Funding,* the FBI data bank, and credit-bureau abuses?

A favorite expression of people who attempt to delineate a goal for programming is the "amplification of human intelligence." It is a fact of life today that even as lofty a goal as this would not be able to lay claim to anything like universal approval. A new Ludditism has arisen in the land, and the computer is taking much of the brunt of its wrath. Unlike their 19th-century counterparts, today's Luddites have not yet begun an organized campaign to smash the machines. Nevertheless, it is certainly true that programmers stand accused in the eyes of many of making a large contribution to the bewilderment of modern life. We ourselves cannot fault as lofty a goal as amplifying human intelligence; we have great confidence in human intelligence. But we feel that it is necessary to ask to what end?

* See note on page 31.

The goal of programming, then, is to write better programs which amplify our intelligence and provide better information for everyone so that . . . . What? (Of course, when we get to this point, doctoring has the same problem: better health for everyone so that . . . . What?)

Methodology. Programming has for all practical purposes no methodology, at least none which would pass the lightest scientific, engineering, or even literary scrutiny, or even our own scrutiny if we are honest about it. When faced with a programming problem ask yourself: are you more likely to review the literature or dig in and solve it yourself? Reviewing the literature is considered such bad form in most programming shops that one dare not be caught reading a book when one is supposed to be working, unless it is a software manual.

Professional forum. Toulmin distinguishes between "compact," "diffuse," and "would-be" disciplines. A compact discipline is a "rational enterprise whose conceptual repertory is exposed at every stage to critical reappraisal and modification by qualified judges, in the light of clearly recognized and agreed collective ideals."[6] Programming is clearly not yet a compact discipline. It is, in fact, currently characterized by rampant variations and poor, nonexistent, or skewed selection processes. Toulmin believes that the shortcomings of diffuse and would-be disciplines are usually either methodological or institutional or both. Such disciplines lack a clearly defined and generally agreed on reservoir of problems because of their failure to develop properly analyzed disciplinary goals or because they lack a suitable professional forum in which to critically test innovations directed toward the achievement of such goals.

The "invisible colleges" of the sciences, "whose members are in close personal contact, study each other's work, and engage in a respectful but competitive rivalry," function formally and informally as a professional forum for those disciplines.[7] A discussion of the institutional problems which militate against the development of something analogous in programming would require an in-depth analysis of International Business Machines and its impact on the profession. Such an analysis is not within the scope of this discussion. The complex problems of legitimate authority, viable journals, and critical forums are complicated by the fact that IBM has a strong economic interest in the direction programming takes, with the result that the evolution of the discipline is not solely in the hands of its practitioners (programmers) but is also influenced by planners, antitrust lawyers, marketing representatives, field engineers, and accountants. Our considered view is that while IBM's contributions to American technology and business have been enormous and constructive, it may not have been doing all that it could to encourage the development of a well-integrated programming profession.

AS THE WORLD TURNS

Established institutions present a kind of paradox. They are necessary to carry a discipline forward—they are to a large degree entrusted with the discipline's traditions (or "transmit," to use Toulmin's term)—but they can also serve to stifle innovation. It almost seems sometimes that therein lies the meaning of "established." The important point is that the merits of an innovation must be judged on its suitability to the solution of outstanding problems, not on its lineage. A useful innovation may come from the scientific side or the technological side, or may be derived from investigations much further afield.

Toulmin observes that in technology the relative pace of innovation may be explained "partly by internal disciplinary considerations (e.g., the comparative 'ripeness' of different problems), partly by the external influence of the market."[8]

EXERCISE FOR STUDENTS

Can you think of an example of a hinderance to innovation in programming? Can you think of more than one? (If so, why have you been quiet so long?)

Certain aspects of computer technology could enhance the possibilities for the effective and speedy development of variation. Evolution is a two-stage process: (1) the appearance of novel variants, and (2) the selection from among those variants into, in our case, the repertory of a discipline. In this second stage, computers can serve as the medium of communication as well as the target of innovation. In fact, programming could provide the model of a modern professional forum.

A short scenario will illustrate: A graduate student has used a computer to explore an analogy between certain phenomena observed in paleontology and certain phenomena observed in programming. This exploration reveals that the paleontological analogy has (in the student's opinion) an important bearing on some outstanding problem of the programming profession. As things now stand, the student would spend 2 years struggling to get the thesis in print, after which it would be microfilmed, filed, and forgotten. However, if the programming profession were in the habit of having monthly teleconferences via computer network, our graduate student would be able to go through certain screening processes and get a slot to present these findings during the next teleconference.

A number of screening routes should be available—approval, petition, or appeal—thus providing ways of short-circuiting the conservative influence of established institutions when necessary. At the monthly conference, the variation would be presented for criticism and possible selection into the repertory of the profession. This method could accelerate the rate of development in the profession as well as provide a prototypical communication system for other disciplines.

ART IS A GOOD INVESTMENT, BUT ARTISTS ARE NOT

Although both art and science spring from the same array of cultural values, they differ in that artistic goals vary widely among individual artists. Continuity resides mainly in a commonly held body of techniques (such as piano playing or brush wielding). The continuity of the sciences includes, as we have noted, a collective body of goals as well.[9]

Programming is often called an art. Sometimes this is intended as a complaint, and sometimes it is not. As Weinberg points out, it is very easy for a programmer to conceal what he or she is up to. Consequently, it is often difficult to determine whether individual artistic goals are being pursued or the collective goals that management is pushing. Managers don't want programmers to be artists. Virtuosity in technique they like, but independent setting of goals they don't.

Managers are not really interested in scientists either. Between Artist and Scientist, management generally would prefer neither. Unflavored programmers would be a manager's dream. Scientists and artists are very difficult to motivate with respect to business objectives; they never figure out exactly what it is the accountants do, they are too mobile, and they have strong allegiances to personal (artistic) or disciplinary (scientific) goals that often outweigh their allegiance to profit. Still, programming will persist as an art and grow as a science (we hope), and though rare is the company that can really afford scientists or artists in their midst, there are some, and that is a good thing.

PROGRAM IT AGAIN, SAM

In this book, we want to examine the nature of the programming paradigm—the set of basic assumptions in the name of which the whole enterprise is carried off. Many readers, we expect, will be surprised to learn that programming has any assumptions whatever; certainly most of us would be hard put to say what they are.

Toulmin tells us that agreement on a set of fundamental concepts or set of presuppositions signifies that an undertaking has achieved disciplinary status. Therefore, in order to get things started, we propose to propose some. Henceforth, let it be known among all programmers that:

1. Language is a part of nature.
2. Language may be hosted in digital storage.
3. Programming is supposed to make digital storage useful.

TWO

A LITTLE HISTORY

THE TRANSMIT

Every discipline has a body of assumptions, techniques, and goals that is passed from generation to generation of practitioners. Toulmin calls such an evolving body of concepts a "transmit."[1] In addition to preserving a discipline through successive generations, the transmit provides a means for evaluating prospective newcomers. By demonstrating mastery of this common inheritance, an apprentice establishes the right to membership in a profession.

A transmit, like a biological species, is not static; it evolves over time. New variations or innovations in assumptions, techniques, or goals appear; if useful, they are selected in and adopted, while older, no longer useful elements are selected out, or dropped. Take doctoring. Western medicine as practiced today is very different from medicine as practiced 100 or 1000 years ago. There is, nevertheless, a clear conceptual genealogy of evolving attitudes, practices, and beliefs, which can be traced back from the present through teacher and student, apprentice and practitioner, to Hippocrates, 400 years before Christ.

We must also understand that no transmit, or discipline,

exists in a vacuum. A transmit must be seen in terms of its interaction with the transmits of other disciplines, related and unrelated, and in terms of interaction with the larger encompassing transmit belonging to all members of Western civilization. This larger, generally held body of assumptions, techniques, and goals is more usually referred to as "the culture" or "tradition." We prefer to use the word "transmit" (although here we are considerably expanding Toulmin's use of the term) because it emphasizes the crucial point that what we are talking about is not static but ever-changing. The culture evolves. The influence of the larger transmit is particularly important in understanding a technological discipline like computer programming because, as we have already noted, such disciplines are heavily influenced in their development by considerations of the marketplace and public opinion as well as by the efforts of the members of the profession themselves.

The programming transmit is as yet both rudimentary and imperfectly perceived, which has had an adverse effect on the definition of goals and the determination of ways to achieve them. Programming is a relatively young discipline, which accounts in part for the thinness of its transmit. There has been considerable difficulty developing a methodology and figuring out how to facilitate its acquisition by apprentice programmers. Even more constraining is the fact that members of the profession generally fail to see any connection between their discipline and the culture.

In addition, programmers are mostly oblivious to the fact that underlying both the design and the widespread use of computers are fundamental assumptions about the human race and the universe. The assumptions of the programming transmit require close scrutiny (with an eye toward possible revision) if we are to make any sense of where we are and where we are going. Where we *are* is in considerable difficulty. Problems with software are commonplace in every part of life the computer touches. Everyone in the profession knows that software is expensive, unreliable, difficult to develop on schedule, nearly impossible to test, and extremely troublesome to maintain. Getting the job done at all nearly always takes precedence over getting the job done right.

TROUBLED WATER

If you have worked in the real world, you know how a manager would react if a programmer brought up such fundamental matters as what assumptions about the human race and the universe a program is making. A good systems programmer must be a jackleg carpenter, and jackleg carpenters do not usually read philosophy, although more and more they are coming to read the *CoEvolution Quarterly.* "Design things right the first time," "professionalism," "publish our results" will all likely mean the same thing to a programming manager: goofing off. In one sense this is correct, of course. The manager wants to get the job done and rightly understands that if there isn't someone keen on getting the job done, the job will not get done. Yet all these efforts to get–the–job–done tend to work against Getting The Job Done.

An associative machine can think about everything at once by using a search argument of all DON'T CAREs. It may also think about nothing at once by using a search argument of all DOESN'T OCCURs. Thus we may think about everything or nothing, but neither will do us much good. It is the intermediate sets we are able to think about simultaneously that we have found to be to our advantage. The sets we characteristically think about seem to have evolved, and so have the sets our machines are thinking about, although in a rather peculiar fashion.

We propose a reexamination of the assumptions of programming, and we intend to suggest some changes in those assumptions in terms of both methodology and goals. Assumptions evolve, and unless we are aware of them, we will have no influence on their development. Present assumptions about computer use in general and the computer industry in particular are limiting the ways in which the computer could be used. Worse yet, some of those assumptions are badly out of step with the American traditions of privacy and individuality.

We know enough about evolution to use that knowledge in design work (e.g., breeding hybrid corn). We need a little conscious design effort applied to the evolution of our concepts, sets, or whatever; herein clearly lies the answer to the current problems with software as well as the foundations for what the Japanese (and some others) call "Information Society." Japan has billions of yen allocated in this area between now and 1985.[2]

Taking a position at all critical of technology exposes us to the hazard of being labeled hopeless romantics, irrationalists, or Luddities. To clear this up early, we assert that technology is a part of nature (as what isn't?) and that although the problems technology creates are real and threatening, they won't be solved either by destroying computers or by ignoring them and moving back to the woods. Buckminster Fuller says don't fight forces, use them.[3] This is sound advice.

It is also important to note that what will be espoused here is not irrationalism. However, we shall construe rational behavior more broadly than simply logical behavior. This may, in fact, provide a line of defense against irrationalism (although, of course, there is no way to reason with an irrationalist) because deductive logic and the hypothetico-mathematical tradition are often set up as straw men for the irrationalists to attack. We are set upon expanding rationalism, not attacking it.

Shortly before the Wright brothers' first flight, it had been proved that motorized flight was impossible. The proof was rigorous and convincing. The wings, in order to supply sufficient lift for the engine, would themselves add such additional weight (requiring a bigger engine, requiring in turn even bigger wings, and so on) that getting off the ground would be impossible.

However, the proof assumed solid wings. New assumptions, for which bicycle technology supplied the key, provided the solution.[4] Similarly, there is conclusive proof that the problems with software have no solution. There will never be enough money, or enough time, or enough programmers.

EXERCISE FOR STUDENTS

Cycle down to North Carolina. Stand on the high dune at Kitty Hawk. Note the strong breeze from seaward.

Kenner: "Being restricted in bandwidth, each of our senses resembles a radio and whatever is infra or ultra to man's sensory tuning . . . we tend to discount as imperfectly real."[5] As we amplify our powers with instrumentation made feasible by computer technology, we will not only accelerate the race toward the future but will likely encourage a reassessment of the long past as well. Humanity would do well to have a good handle on the latter before getting too carried away with the former.

BIRTH OF THE ALU

It is not realistic to expect every mathematician to read the history of mathematics or every engineer to study the history of mining, but it is realistic to expect practitioners of a discipline to at least be aware that there *is* a history of what they are doing. In the case of programming, that history reaches back at least several hundred years.

We have said that our transmit is imperfectly perceived. This is evident in the way in which the history of computer technology is usually set forth. Most accounts emphasize the history of computation and ignore the informational tradition advancing through Jacquard's loom and Vaucanson's duck ("a gilded copper automaton which 'drinks, eats, quacks, splashes about on water, and digests his food like a living duck' "[6]). Instead, most histories begin with some odometer builder, say Pope Gregory I or Pascal, and then leap approximately to Von Neumann, with a brief stop-off for Babbage and Turing. Emphasizing computation and ignoring memory, this version leaves half the story untold.

Although the calculating machine may be said to have fathered the modern computer, the barrel organ mothered it. The major historical importance of Babbage's machine lies in the fact that it marked the convergence of computational technology with a more general informational technology. This second branch of the computer's ancestral tree stretches back at least to 14th-century medieval Europe and involves the technologies of weaving, musical automata, and mechanical clocks.

Developing out of water-clock technology and the astrolabe (an instrument for navigating by the stars), the invention of the mechanical clock was one of the remarkable achievements of medieval Europe. For thousands of years the human race had observed the passage of time in the alternations of day and night, the changing seasons, and the movements of the stars and planets in relation to the earth. In the 14th century, massive tower clocks, marking the hours with carillons played by huge barrel-organ cylinders, began to ornament city halls and palaces.

The clocks were designed as "exhibitions of the pattern of the cosmos," an analog of the universe; they kept track of all aspects of time.[7] The circular face represented the equinoctial circle. Various other signs, symbols, and figures indicated the day, date, religious festivals, and movements of the planets, as well as solar, lunar, and sidereal time (time measured by the rotation of the earth in relation to the stars). The clocks quickly captured the imagination of the public. Lynn White says: "No European community felt able to hold up its head unless in its midst the planets wheeled in cycles and epicycles, while angels trumpeted, cocks crew, and apostles, kings, and prophets marched and countermarched at the booming of the hours."[8]

The earliest mechanical clocks were powered by a weight-driven mechanism which had the disadvantage of delivering energy in a continually decreasing flow (by Newton's third law). The problem was solved by the invention of the escapement, a device to control the flow of energy by releasing it in units that were separate and more or less equal. The escapement improved accuracy and at the same time reduced the measurement of the passage of time to discrete units, thus apparently digitizing time (although it wasn't until the middle of the 17th century that minutes were marked on the clock face). As clock technology developed over the next 3 centuries, increasing attention was paid to improving accuracy and precision in the representation of discrete units of time and less and less to modeling the universe. The culmination of this transformation is the present-day digital readout clock, whose designers have eliminated the last remnant of the analog time machine—its circular face.

Lewis Mumford described the clock as the "key-machine" of the modern industrial age and considered its invention more significant than that of the steam engine.

> The clock, moreover, is a piece of power-machinery whose "product" is seconds and minutes: by its essential nature it dissociated time from human events and helped create the belief in an independent world of mathematically measurable sequences: the special world of science.[9]

It is true that most of the uses to which the measurement of time are put today do not require attention to the movements of the planets around the sun or even specifically to sunrise and sunset. Universal acceptance of particular conventions in time telling and accuracy to fractions of a second are more useful and important. Nevertheless, it would be well to remember that however artificial the framework of time we have imposed on ourselves, it is still the relationship of the earth to the rest of the universe that we are measuring; those long-vanished analog devices whose gears, dials, and moving figures represented that relationship to medieval people still persist in some ghostly fashion, continuing their stately delineation of the pattern of the cosmos behind the square face of a push-button digital wrist watch.

EXERCISE FOR STUDENTS

What relationship does the STIMER macro bear to the music of the spheres?

The barrel organ, like the clock, has a long and venerable history. Its best-known modern descendant is the simple crank-operated mechanical instrument once played by itinerant street musicians or their trained monkeys (Babbage found them enormously irritating). Barrel organs first appeared in Western Europe in the 14th century. They were used to play the carillons whose chiming marked the time kept by the massive tower clocks. The heart of the barrel organ is a wooden or metal cylinder studded with pegs or staples in particular arrangements. As the barrel is turned (driven by the clock's machinery), the pegs activate levers connected to bells or pipes, producing musical notes.

As the technology advanced, making a reduction in size possible, self-playing instruments incorporating the barrel-organ cylinder and clockwork machinery were made for homes and churches; by the 16th century, music was being composed especially for such instruments. In the 18th century, scholarly books were written on the art of cylinder pinning. The aim of that art was "to reproduce with absolute precision the execution of the music as intended by its composer."[10]

By the 19th century, the cylinder had been replaced by

punched cardboard strips, which were easier and less expensive to produce and made an increased repertory more practical. This change apparently came after the punched card innovations in the weaving industry which culminated in the Jacquard loom in about 1804. However, interrelationships between automatic musical instruments and weaving technology existed at least from the 16th-century partnership of the German composer Hassler and the weaver G. Heinlein, who together constructed a mechanical organ and sold it to Rudolph II of Bavaria.[11]

Automatic musical instruments probably reached their zenith in the 1920s with the development of complex and sophisticated "recording pianos" by the American Piano Company (Ampico), the Aeolian Company (Duo-Art), and the Auto-Pneumatic Action Company (Welte-Mignon). Performances by such artists as Paderewski, Rachmaninoff, and Horowitz were recorded on paper rolls and marketed to be played on pianos equipped with reproducing player devices on which the full range of piano dynamics could be duplicated. According to Ampico's historian, Larry Givens, "virtually every pianist of renown who was active during the first three decades of this century made recordings for these pianos."[12]

The reproducing mechanisms were installed in various makes of piano built either by the player manufacturers themselves or by traditional piano builders such as Steinway and Stroud. The commercial success of the reproducing piano was cut short by the Depression and the development of the radio and phonograph. Although these elegant instruments are still available, the player-piano music one finds most commonly today in pizza parlors and bars is only a weak echo of a Steinway equipped with the mechanism to "reenact" a performance by Rachmaninoff.

Mechanical music and weaving technology, like the printing press, embody the human desire to record and reproduce satisfying and useful patterns in the absence of the patternmaker. The carillon, music box, and reproducing piano are all machines for the mechanical storage and retrieval of information. The earliest barrel-organ cylinders reproduced pitch and the sequence of notes, but the music lacked expression. As the technology of pinning cylinders improved, it became possible to add subtle variations in tempo, phrasing, and tone quality, which resulted in a performance more nearly approximating that of a live musician. On a well-pinned cylinder, the pins stored both notes and expression. This capability has been largely lost in present-day computer programming.

WEAVE IT AGAIN, SAM

Modern science (very modern on a time scale which includes the Stone Age) has created as many problems as it has solved. We do not refer here to the problem of beer cans along highways but to the domination of thought by the formal and systematic aspects of the hypothetico-deductive method, a domination which has been both constraining and distorting. When thought to be the only way or the ideal way, this tradition hampers or prohibits the exploration of many useful avenues of investigation; because of its reliance on the abstract symbols of mathematics, it has distorted our view of the relationship of language to the world and hence distorted our view of ourselves.

Modern computers have accelerated the trend toward formalism and have enhanced its specious primacy because of the amenability of the old formalism to digital storage organized around an arithmetic logic unit (ALU) Storage was used to play music long before it was used to hold algorithms. Massive digital storage is a resource which need not be organized around an ALU but may be used in other ways.

Computer models are programs which purport to work as the world works. They are constructed on the doctrine that all useful explanation can ultimately be stated in formal terms; that is, all useful explanation can be described by an algorithm, obeys two-valued logic, is discrete, can be precisely represented by mathematical symbols, and so on. Exceptions are considered to be either insufficiently advanced as yet or simply not useful or rational. It is implicit in this doctrine that the ultimate aim is to incorporate all science into one body of explanation whose relationships will all be statable in terms of mathematical logic.

If you look at how the world actually works, you will see that reality flows. The distinction between continuous and discrete is arbitrary; any attempt to impose a continuous/discrete dualism may seem tidy at first but on closer examination reveals perplexing ambiguity. Still, "continuous" or "analog" best describes what reality is like, and "discrete" or "digital" best describes what thinking is like—at least formal thinking and certainly machine thinking. Originally, when a person wanted to measure something, an analog method was used. Discreteness was only a convention imposed on analog mechanisms, like inches on a yardstick, to facilitate replication and communication. A computer is a kind of high-order convention capable of being imposed on a wide and various assortment of analog mechanisms. But reality still flows.

The clock escapement (an early flip-flop) imposed a discrete organization on a continuous process. In time, the discrete became predominant. We must now find techniques to impose continuous processes back on discrete (digital) storage, as prehistoric humans learned to do when they shifted toolmaking technology from flaking stone to grinding stone. The sources of solutions to these problems are diverse, but the purpose is singular: to make electronic digital storage more useful.

The extent and homogeneity of the digital storage resource can eliminate the need for formal rigor as a means of modifying, organizing, and transmitting knowledge. Knowledge can be stored and accessed in utterly new ways ranging from the old way to any old way. Only one thing holds us back: programming. We must devise ways of mapping the continuous world into digital storage—and more important, useful ways of mapping it back—in nonformal and informal ways, using a notation which is no longer confined to marks on paper or holes in cards.

We envision that when scientific explanation is no longer bound to deductive inference and particulate notation, it will reconverge with its origins in natural language after a 2000-year digression into formalism. The development of a technology for the proper use of digital storage is the key. Proper model building with human/machine ensembles is the beginning.

EXERCISE FOR STUDENTS

Hide the ALU from your commune's minicomputer. Tell the others that you have had a vision, that the Great Spirit has willed the people not to add, neither to sort, and so on. Then use the storage as an electric grandmother.

THREE

MAKING TOOLS FROM DIGITAL STORAGE

THE ALLEGORY OF THE PREPLATONIC CAVE

The phenomenon of a transmit—which persists independently of the life and death of any individual—requires the use of symbols. Symbolic activity is not different in kind from other human behavior; it is merely a particular sort of activity which can be usefully identified and talked about. Symbol manipulation is part of a web of adaptive behavior. The web is seamless; it includes symbol use and tool use, and the computer combines these two in a unique way.

We know from cave paintings that humans were already symbol users thousands of years ago, although little other direct evidence of symbolic behavior seems to have survived the glaciers. Symbols enable us to work with information instead of the actual resource that the symbols represent. Just so with the prehistoric painter:

> Clearly, it was the *act* of *painting* that counted. The painter had to go way down in the most mysterious depths of the earth and create an animal in paint. Possibly he believed that by doing this he gained some sort of magic power over the same kind of

> animal when he hunted it in the open air. It certainly doesn't look as if he cared very much about the picture he painted—as a finished product to be admired—for he or somebody else soon went down and painted another animal right over the one he had done.[1]

The programmer and the discipline of programming have come close to realizing humanity's ancient dream of making things obey symbols. The prehistoric painter presages the day when cattle in a feedlot are manipulated by tax-evasion specialists looking at computer printouts (no dung on their boots, no telling scars of the hunt). One way to make things obey your symbols is to make the things yourself.

We have designed that long-ago vision into partial reality. Information is the essence of design, but it has for all practical purposes remained transparent. Now, however, we have come to the point where we wish to design information itself. Thus we must have information about information; we must somehow undo the transparency.

EXERCISE FOR STUDENTS
(Extra credit)

Go deep into a cave; perform rites on information. (You have to start somewhere.)

Let's paint a little picture of information on the wall here, with the understanding that others will paint over it as we come to understand our subject better. Information is a symbolic representation of some perception of an aspect of the world. The symbols may be numbers, formulas, words, music, photographs, or drawings. They may be in a form perceptible to any or all of the senses. Organized into a sentence, a table of figures, or a musical score, the symbols represent an interpretation of some aspect of the world. Information facilitates the organization of resources by making possible experimental manipulation of the symbols rather than the actual resources. This has the obvious advantage of being more economical of time, energy, and the resources themselves. Information, by this definition, is the medium by which we record, store, and communicate our sense of the world to each other.

Two varieties of problems arise in the use of information. First, it is frequently overlooked that the usefulness of the information depends on the quality of the symbols used. Little boxes scaled to represent the size of individual pieces of furniture leave out color, texture, and degree of hardness, which may limit their usefulness in arriving at a satisfying room arrangement. Numbers representing people leave out quite a lot. To avoid serious misrepresentations of reality, it is important to keep in mind the limitations of the symbols one has chosen to use. Second, just as in programming, where the address is sometimes confused with the data stored there, people who manipulate information sometimes forget that they are not handling the actual resource.

It may be that organizations of the future will have to implement some kind of informational audit, applying certain tests to ensure that what is being passed about as information has in fact some statable relationship to reality. Equity Funding Corp., we feel, has set important precedents here.* The fact that their objective was fraud should not distract us from the pioneering work

* The management of Equity Funding Corp. of America, a company which sold both mutual-fund shares and life insurance, inserted records for nonexistent policyholders into the company's computerized record-keeping system in order to provide evidence of growing assets. As pressure on the company grew, the policies were sold to reinsurers to provide cash. At intervals, the nonexistent policyholders were killed off and death benefits were collected from the reinsuring companies to pay the premiums on new additions to the list of nonexistent policyholders. By the time the conspiracy collapsed in 1973, 64,000 of the 97,000 policyholders recorded in Equity Funding's computers were nonexistent people. For a more detailed description of the swindle, see Thomas Whiteside, *Computer Capers: Tales of Electronic Thievery, Embezzlement and Fraud,* New York, Crowell, 1978, Chapter 2.

they did in information technology. They knew what the relationship of their information to reality was, which is a lot more than can be said for many honest enterprises. (Fuller feels that innovation frequently stems from outlawry, although he seems to have a somewhat more romantic notion of outlaw in mind than the thieves at Equity Funding.)

Meanwhile, back in the cave, another phenomenon. A different ancient person, this one ahead of the times, is drawing a person drawing an animal. Here you get the flavor of the abstract nature of the information used at the top of a large organization. Hark! There is a person drawing a person drawing a person drawing an animal. That person is the earliest known information theorist. Is there yet another ancient person drawing?

It is important to note that in trying to understand information, we are not necessarily looking for principles which already exist but are simply trying to find new and more useful ways of looking at things. The Pythagoreans believed that mathematics reflected the design of the universe (God is a geometer). By the operation of pure thought, of which mathematics was held to be the essence, they were convinced that the workings of the world could be deduced. This belief in the preexistence of a mathematical design led eventually to a loss of mathematical power. Concepts are not immutable properties of physical reality or of ourselves, but instead are useful ways of looking at things—tools or instruments we design and use to shape the interface between ourselves and the not-ourselves in pursuit of our goals.

YES OR NO

The reader will notice that our definition of information does not include the notion of "bits." Shannon defines the bit as the choice between plus or minus—the amount of information needed to remove the uncertainty between yes and no. Shannon's original interest was in switching theory. He developed equations to express the behavior of switches mathematically and then showed that his equations could be manipulated by a calculus isomorphic with the propositional calculus of symbolic logic, that is, Boolean algebra.

Shannon himself was very skeptical about the applicability of his theories to the other diverse disciplines which immediately took them up (only to drop them years later after much unproductive work). His theories applied to the problem they were tailored to, and, or course, they also applied very well to digital computing. Thus it is not a question of where Shannon went wrong, for Shannon went right—very right. His rightness lies in a well-tailored solution to a well-defined problem.

Shannon said: "The fundamental problem of communication is that of reproducing at one point either exactly or approximately a message selected at another point. Frequently the messages have *meaning* . . . These semantic aspects are irrelevant to the engineering problem."[2]

We cannot blame him for not solving problems he did not address. The question is whether his theory provides an adequate metaphor for illuminating the characteristics of information as we have defined it. We believe that it does not. A distinction must be made between channel capacity and information content. Shannon has provided us with a useful model of channel capacity; engineers use it in designing communication networks. However, Shannon's model does not provide any measure of information content—only symbol capacity—and this severely restricts its use. It follows, then, that the bit is a mechanical part of the symbol system used in switching theory (and in computers). It, in conjunction with other bits, carries information in binary code, but it is not itself information. Nor is it a useful unit of measurement of information as we have defined it, any more than the number of letters used could measure the information contained on a printed page.

What happens to information in a computer? Where are the

connotations of love while the word is hosted in a digital store as 11010011110101101110010111000101? The connotations of the word "love" remain in the culture, and they flow back when the word is retrieved from the store for some purpose. It is clear, then, that when we are manipulating symbols in a digital machine, we are not manipulating meanings but rather their inert hosts. Only when we retrieve symbols from the machine do they impinge once again on the culture.

THE ULTIMATE STONE AGE COMPUTER

The first stone tools used by prehistoric people were probably rocks that already happened to have a useful cutting edge. Later, they learned to make their own tools by breaking flakes off a stone in a way that left a useful edge. Flaking worked best with flint, and the technique was gradually improved over thousands of years until, just before the change to grinding, it had reached a stage of such delicacy that their tools are now called "microliths."[3] Mesolithic people learned to chip very small blades from a prepared core of flint. These little blades, shaped into triangles, half-moons, or trapezoids, were the cutting edges attached to a haft of bone or wood to form implements and weapons. This technique provided a more economical use of the limited supply of flint available.

The microliths—finely wrought stone blades in various geometric shapes—were the end and highest product of the flaked-stone period, when humans hunted, gathered, and fished. Their appearance came just before a basic change in human life, when people began to cultivate food instead of foraging. This change called forth a new technique in toolmaking. Implements began to be shaped by grinding stone instead of flaking it, enabling formation of the heavy durable tools required to clear forests and cultivate land. Note that technology developed to fill a need.

This was a major technological breakthrough: A distinctly discrete technique (flaking) was replaced by a more nearly continuous technique (grinding) to impose, in effect, a continuous interface. Similar broad-brush techniques must arise to shape digital storage to human needs. In the near future, programs of several hundred trillion bytes will be common. Clearly, little individual attention will be paid to any given bit; large aggregates of bits (*big bits*) will be shaped, or such programs will not exist. Machine programming—programs writing programs—will naturally play a major role; grinding rock is done with other rocks.

Grinding stone also meant that using flint or obsidian was no longer necessary. Baser rock could be ground to serve as well as or better than the microliths of the late flaking tradition. Big bits will permit the use of baser programmers, so to speak (digital storage is not scarce, like obsidian; it is plentiful, like space). Big bits will permit the less dexterous to build. Digital storage was, in fact, conceived in a tradition meant to enhance, supplement, and sometimes supplant human dexterity: the barrel organ, the music box, Jacquard's loom.

EXERCISE FOR STUDENTS

It is not too early to get big bits into the mainstream. Mention them a lot; act as if you knew what they are. As Arlo says, if enough people are saying it, pretty soon people will begin to believe it.

Willis Ware, in a 1972 article entitled "The Ultimate Computer," took a broad look at current computers and foresaw that computing power will be increased through improved componentry (miniaturization) and architecture (parallel processing) and that such improved computers would have sufficient power to, for example, model the ocean.[4] He estimated that to build such a computer would cost about half what an Apollo space shot cost.

There seems no reason to doubt Ware's assessment of the potential and cost of current technology. Still, in pointing out the upper limits of computational power, however immense, Ware has also brought into relief the limitations of current techniques for working digital storage. FORTRAN and other current programming languages can be considered the equivalent of early techniques in the Stone Age; writing FORTRAN is a discrete, imprecise, *ad hoc* process, as was flaking stone. The result with both is a somewhat useful edge arrived at partially by chance, with serious structural weaknesses and limited applicability. Stoneworking overcame these shortcomings by grinding: applying a continuous process to obtain a more nearly continuous interface between shaped substance and the world and goals. What is construed to be the interface is arbitrary, but it is not immaterial with regard to usefulness toward achieving goals.

The history of computer architecture from sand tablets, abacus, and odometer through Babbage, Turing, and Von Neumann may be compared to the development of techniques for affixing crude bone hafts to early stone blades to create a more useful tool. Mining and refining digital storage (the blade itself) proceeds apace, from barrel-organ cylinders, music boxes, and looms through punched cards, magnetic disks, and holograms. Soon there will be more of it than we can ever use, but improved hafts continue to elude us. Many explanations can be given, but two seem most helpful:

1. We are being limited by our own preconceptions. Tradition, which is in one sense necessary, is in another sense constraining.

2. We do not yet fully understand the properties of the resource (digital storage) at our disposal.

Limiting preconceptions and lack of understanding will most likely give way with extensive experience. Thus, making digital storage widely available (in big bits for little fingers to play) to facilitate the necessary experience gaining is a top professional priority. Instead of stone we have digital storage—a vast, monolithic, homogeneous, plentiful resource.

SEARCH FOR A SOFTWARE SPOKE

Humankind was held back by the notion that strength entailed weight. We now know that there is far greater strength in structure than in weight—for example, the bicycle spoke.[5] Mankind is now held back by an analogous mistake: Marvelously useful *n*-dimensional digital stores are used as stacks or heaps. There must be structural strength in digital storage, like grain in wood or the locked angle. We cannot arrive at this structure *a priori,* for the property we are looking for is synergistic. Thus we must experiment.

Software is a set of conventions according to which a computing system is arranged. A static description is called "architecture"; a dynamic description is called a "program." These distinctions are arbitrary but not immaterial. Software may be stored in any of the ordinary ways used for storing conventions: written on paper, embodied in the physical relationship of things, stored in magnetic pulses, or remembered in the head.

The way software is designed currently is fundamentally unsound. It is mostly done *ad hoc,* and the underlying assumptions go unrecognized. Fuller says that all technology models principles.[6] Think about this next time you are asked to join a group of fourteen people hammering out the format of a large system or a file for information retrieval. It will, of course, be an all-day meeting. In the morning, deliver yourself of the opinion that all technology models principles. You will find that the afternoon session has been moved to another room and that you have not been told the new room number. Why?

Data formats as we know and love them do not model principles; they model other data formats. The only fields in a data format that seem somehow to be in tune with any (unknown) principles of information are those marked "reserved for future use." Like the unused places of place notation, these alone seem pure. One suspects why: Digital storage is a vessel in which to put (and in which to grow). Suffice it to say that data technology does not currently model any information principles. Where it does, it is modeling compression—a lesser principle (stack it up)—not tension (associations and interrelationships)—a greater principle. Why? Because we do not yet understand the tensional principles of information.

BIG-BIT CHAINS

With the software template we currently impose on n-dimensional homogeneous digital storage, there are only two ways to find something:

1. Look for it
2. Look for it earlier on and remember where it is, with the corollaries:
   a. Put it in a special place and remember where you put it, and
   b. Select the special place to put it so that it can be computed instead of remembered

These constraints on digital storage exist because we do not utilize internal structure of any kind except to note whether a bit is on or off. We impose instead an external structure taken generally from the discipline of filing.

But if information were stored in the orientation of a bit

(especially a big bit) with respect to its neighbors, as well as in whether it is on or off, then, retrieval becomes a matter of extracting a chain from among many by programmed resolution of which filaments connect which nodes. Note that filament resolution will extract a structure based on the bit *orientations* at the nodes; data will still reside in the on-off of the bits. What is envisioned with such bit chains is much broader than anything in use now.

Semantic nets are natural language words in storage which are associated with gradated lists pointing to other words which are in turn associated with lists, and so on. Semantic nets may be the first stone axes of electronic storage, but the overhead of lists of pointers is a clumsy imposition on a homogeneous medium. Semantic nets lack elegance and precision because the words, which are continuous and infinite, are presumed to be discrete and finite for the purpose of being associated with a list.

It is instructive to turn to Samuel Johnson's definition of network here: "*net* and *work*. Any thing reticulated or decussated at equal distances, with interstices between the intersections." Johnson's definition emphasizes the holes as much as the filaments. This is an important point. Shouting "Gotcha covered!" while wielding a net involves certain assumptions; a lot depends on the size of the holes. If our goal is to broaden and flex awareness rather than make it narrow and rigid, we must remain aware of what is slipping through.

The most elegant organization in an *n*-dimensional bit matrix will be a bit chain. How such a chain could be constructed was not previously clear; one bit can only carry one bit of information, after all—not nearly enough to point to the next bit in the chain. However, big bits will enhance our dexterity. A big bit may have *n* neighbors. It contains a list of pointers to all of them (and they all in turn point to it); it also contains flags to indicate whether it is bound to a particular neighbor—whether a filament exists. It is the organization—the context that will determine the context of everything else—that will determine how much and what information a bit carries.

The important point is that we may now search for structure independent of addresses and data. An associative search radiating out from any node will rapidly gather in the pattern which the filaments form, whereas an iterative search would take too long to achieve the same purpose. This search will not be comparative but, as it were, acquisitive, with the programming always looking for nexts with relation to lasts by node rather than comparing wholes to wholes.

BUCKY

A favorite theme of Buckminster Fuller provides a suggestive metaphor. Here is Kenner's version of Fuller speaking in Santa Barbara in 1967:

> Suppose I have a rope between my hands, and I have tied it in an ordinary overhand knot; one rotation 360 degrees, a second rotation 360 degrees, one of them passed through the other. . . .

The knot consists of two circles, which interlock. The relation of the circles is 720 degrees.

> And when I pull the ends of the rope, the knot does not disappear. The knot gets tighter. Each loop prevents the other loop from disappearing. So the knot is a pattern in the rope, and it's a *self-interfering pattern.* The harder I pull, the more the knot stays there.[7]

Interlocking 360-degree orientations link bit to successive bit in a chain. This can be emulated with a standard memory and a programmed template to identify the memory knots. Eventually, the capability will be engineered into storage or implemented with big bits of microcode.

EXERCISE FOR STUDENTS

Design a big bit. Make a chain of big bits. Tie it in a knot.

We may loosen the knot and slip it along the rope, feeding the rope through the pattern. This illustrates two important points: (1) The knot isn't the rope but rather a pattern, and so (2) the knot is indifferent to what the rope consists of. Fuller calls it a "self-interfering patterned integrity." For storage, a bit chain isn't bits—isn't 1s or 0s—but a pattern of potential 1s and 0s, a chain of places, if you like, where 1 or 0 may be kept. A bit in an *n*-dimensional matrix may be tied to any of its neighbors. Bit streams may slide through a bit chain like rope through an overhand knot; a bit chain is a content-free structure. Extracting a chain which bears on information we want involves following filaments from node to node among many criss-crossing bit chains. This is a function of instruction space, which is similarly structured so that we have full recursive power.

Let us forget lines with no width joining points with no magnitude to enclose surfaces with no thickness cut from an infinite plane.

> [L]et us consider a real triangle . . . let us construct one. We may use three strips of wood and pin them together. Tongue depressors will do. And we shall discover at once that two joints swivel freely until we connect the third; whereat, suddenly, all three angles become utterly locked. . . . We have invented a device for guaranteeing the integrity of angles, which is no small achievement in a universe where change is normal.[8]

EXERCISE FOR STUDENTS

Write some code to guarantee the integrity of your bit chain.

In three dimensions, the same effect of locking in the angles gives us the geodesic sphere. Such a structure depends on design for its strength, not the building material, just as the meaning of the bit chain depends on the orientation of each node relative to its neighbors, not whether the node is on or off. We equate this data independence with structural strength.

> We've isolated a useful notion: the idea of strength that is designed in, to be distinguished from strength the carpenter hammers in. Design solves problems elegantly, but force imperfectly. Design is weightless; it costs no nails, it costs no wood; it's pure conformity to principles.[9]

Fuller says don't fight forces, use them. Now consider a bit ripped untimely from core. It is a mess from a binary point of view; it must be immediately sampled, amplified, and smoothed in order for us to get the one bit of information we want. In getting the one bit we want, we are clearly throwing a lot away. Is it (can it be made) useful? Clearly, we are fighting forces to save our precious bit. When a bit is first retrieved from core, it may look like this: . We currently grab it, guess whether it is 1 or 0, smooth it and amplify it so that it looks like this: (nice normal bit). What information have we lost besides such things as how many airplanes have flown over, how many power spikes there have been, and so on? Here are some examples of the information we currently rush to obliterate:

1. When the bit was recorded
2. In conjunction with what else the bit was recorded
3. What the bit supplanted

Big bits will not be small; they will remember each state and orientation they have been in and when each state changed. Once we learn to use big bits to host language correctly, structure will be easier to tease out.

It is worthwhile to remember that humans first differentiated metal out of stone and then differentiated the tensional and compressional factors out of metal.[10] Similarly, we differentiate storage out of electricity. We must further differentiate out a structure of tensional and compressional principles for storage and manipulation of information so that digital storage may be put to its best use.

Digital storage can be used merely to host criminal records, just as a chunk of platinum may be used to prop up a post. In neither case are we using the properties of the substance to the fullest advantage, even though each may be serving its limited purpose very well. By analogy to the compressional and tensional properties of metal, digital storage has the properties "state" (1 or 0) and "link" (next bit in the chain). We mean this analogy broadly in that the linking factor is the stronger in digital storage, just as the tensional factor is in metal. "Tension struts held the Wrights' airplane together, and did not break," says Bucky, "thanks to a piece of design familiar to bicycle mechanics but to few other craftsmen."[11]

PRACTICAL EXERCISE FOR STUDENTS

Which craftsmen have the design science to unlock digital storage? Go out and find them.

It will be some time before there are industry seminars on bit chains or big bits. They are currently speculation—our intuitive guess about what techniques will match future methods to future needs. Technology is the explorer/scout; science is the settler/mapmaker. Science depends on technology both for its tools and for its metaphors. New metaphors must arise to guide our approach to better use of digital storage. When we think of wrenching information from data in digital storage, some vague images come to mind:

- teasing, combing
- old-fashioned, loosely coupled trains starting up
- lock-picking tools
- how MacDuff was ripped untimely from his mother's womb
- absolute, sliding stringency governed by the master wrencher-outer, such as sail, wind, and rigging
- picking cotton candy from the machine

LIVING WITH THE HYDROGEN BOND

Consider life as a metaphor. Nature uses a mapping that any programmer could be proud of. The DNA molecule, described by Watson and Crick in 1952, consists of two complementary strands shaped like an elegant winding staircase whose sides are chains of repeating, identical sugar-phosphates and whose steps are alternating pairs of the nucleotides guanine and cytosine and adenine and thymine, with each pair bonded together in the middle of each stairstep by hydrogen. This particular arrangement of atoms, combined according to the rules of chemistry, is the fundamental blueprint of heredity, the repository and transmitter of all genetic information for every living cell from the cells of the simplest bacteria to those of complex human beings.

Nature seems to implement without a preoccupation with Life (chemistry is not life), which leads one strongly to suspect that information can be designed without being preoccupied with Meaning (bits are not concepts). Nature is content to let the rules of base pairing serve her larger purpose (life), and we should be content to let the bit orientations serve our larger purpose (meaning) without cluttering the micro level with macro concepts. It is important to remember this while learning to mind the digital store.

Meaning has a meaningless substructure, just as life has a lifeless substructure. What does all of this mean, if anything? Can bit bonds in mass storage support meaning as hydrogen bonds in matter support life? Clearly, it is at least a more interesting way to look at mass storage than as a large electronic filing cabinet on the one hand or a scratch pad for the intermediate results of calculations of horrendous size on the other.

The analogy of programming technology to the transition from flaking to grinding stone carries the implication that we are nearing a breakthrough, not coming to an end. Prehistorians are at a loss to explain the how and why of the agricultural revolution, but Braidwood's description strongly suggests the applicability of Thom's catastrophe theory: "About ten or twelve thousand years ago, the general level of culture in many parts of the world seems to have been ready for a change."[12] Now, as then, some as–yet–unknown processes are approaching discontinuity. There will be a comparable change in human life accompanying the shift from flaking to grinding in digital storage technology. Perhaps large numbers of people will migrate from the earth. We are confronted with a newly abundant resource—digital storage. We shall make tools of it, as we have done with stone and metal. And, since the shape of the tool to a large degree determines the shape of what we make with it, what sorts of tools shall we make? To what purpose shall we turn knowledge of this substance?

PRACTICAL EXERCISE FOR STUDENTS

1. *Read the Japanese "Plan for Information Society—A National Goal toward Year 2000."*[13]
2. *Plant a tree and think about your grandchildren (who are real people, though perhaps as yet unborn).*

FOUR

THE CHESS PLAYER UNDER THE TABLE

The giant automatons used by early Egyptian priests in religious ceremonies were designed with no attempt to conceal the inner workings or the priest manipulating them—apparently, it was thought that the artifacts were marvelous enough without any dissembling. But later, in Europe, elaborate care was taken to conceal the operating principles of automatons. An automaton built by W. Von Kempelen, which was alleged to play chess but whose complex machinery later was found to be under rather direct human control, was considered to be out of the spirit of the thing.[1] But out of the spirit of what?

Several other questions arise:

1. Can all processes used to manipulate concepts be approximated to within delta, given a powerful enough machine and some suitable extension of the calculus? In other words, can machines think?
2. Since machines may host the processes used to manipulate concepts (given the fact that these processes are concepts themselves and that machines can host all language and hence any attendant concepts), can machines be designed to employ these processes to ac-

tually manipulate concepts without their being made discrete first by approximation? That is, can machines emulate thinking?

3. What is wrong with the Egyptian approach? If we are working toward some commonly agreed on goal (such as pacifying angry gods), the question of dissembling does not arise, only the question: Is the system serving its purpose (are the gods pacified?); that is, isn't it a silly question about machines thinking?

A programmer of our acquaintance was presented with the familiar puzzle "Instant Insanity." Instead of writing a program to solve the puzzle, he wrote a program to narrow the possibilities. The first run narrowed them to about 40,000; a second run narrowed them to 8, and it was a simple matter for the programmer himself to find the solution among these. Cheating? This programmer seemed to feel so because he didn't tell his co-workers that the solution was partly human; he merely presented them with the solution and eight lines of undecipherable PL/I. No one read the code. When he later confessed, this was generally taken to detract from his prowess as a programmer. And since it was a game, perhaps rightly so, because considered as a programming game, human intervention was cheating. Suppose not a game but substantive activity were involved. Would the part-human solution still be considered somehow not in the spirit of things (like Von Kempelen's chess player), even though it had the distinct advantages of a short algorithm and reduced execution time, plus the unknown amount of time saved in not developing the unknown (to the programmer) algorithm for solving the puzzle? One wonders.

REMEMBER DREYFUS'S PAPER? DREYFUS WAS RIGHT

In a 1965 work, "Alchemy and Artificial Intelligence," Hubert Dreyfus attacked the belief that intelligent behavior in human beings differs from intelligent behavior in machines only in degree of complexity.[2] (For Dreyfus's most recent views on the subject, see his "Introduction to the Revised Edition," *What Computers Can't Do*, New York, Harper & Row, 1979, pp. 1–87.) Dreyfus observed that the field of artificial intelligence had followed a recurring pattern. In each new project, early dramatic success was followed by sudden unexpected difficulties. Development of computer systems in general follows this pattern and can be broken down as follows: The formalizable portion of a process is identified and programmed; it then becomes apparent that the process, whatever it is, is not entirely formalizable, but only partly formalizable, and that no consideration has been given to implementing the necessary interface to incorporate humans into the system in order to cover the nonformalizable portion.

We always start off on the wrong foot, thinking that any and every process can be completely formalized. In the case of language translation, early success was with simple lexicography, which was formalizable and easily programmed. Trouble set in when it became evident that grammar was not completely formalizable without reference to context, and chaos resulted when it was realized that machines could never determine context with certainty because they could not grasp the metaphorical extensions of words, assess thinghood, and so on. (According to Dreyfus, five government agencies spent 16 million 1964 dollars on the problem.[3])

There are many things machines can't do; there are even more things they can't do well. Whether this is an inherent problem of machines, as Dreyfus argues, or merely the current state of affairs, one thing is clear: If people and machines work together, many things can be done and done well.

Consider pattern recognition: Not surprisingly, programs can recognize only the patterns they are programmed to recognize. This lends weight to the common belief that machines can do only what they are told to do. Machines can be told to create their own patterns to recognize, which confutes the common belief but has one shortcoming—it is of no particular use. The fact that a machine gets the patterns it recognizes from a human should not be thought to detract from the machine; the question is simply: At what system node should patterns be passed from human to machine? The patterns should not be passed at the programmer-writing-code node but at some user-using-the-system node.

Similarly, discrimination between essential and inessential information is now usually made by programmers at design or, frequently, coding time, whereas a more useful system would permit the user to make this discrimination at use time. As Dreyfus notes, humans are able to function with varying levels of ambiguity (i.e., ambiguity tolerance determined by context), while any formal approach entails fixed ambiguity tolerance or eliminating ambiguity altogether.

Dreyfus argued that there were some areas of intelligent activity which machines could not emulate because such activities require fringe consciousness, essence/accident discrimination, and ambiguity tolerance—functions which digital computers could not provide and "of which the only existing prototype is the little-understood human brain." His arguments are sound, yet RETAIN/370 handles precisely these sorts of functions, and the problem of language translation by computer has been largely solved by LOGOS.*

The salient point is that the system which solved the translation problem is not completely computerized; 95% of the translation is done by machine and 5% by humans, who can provide the element which Dreyfus insisted that machines couldn't provide. Human and machine work together on the translation problem,

* RETAIN/370 is IBM's internal maintenance information system; LOGOS is a system which was originally developed to translate technical manuals from English to Vietnamese.

each doing what it does best. Similarly, humans are a key system element in the RETAIN/370 design. This is the way of the future. The notation problem (the design of the human/machine interface) is the biggest obstacle to developing this kind of system. LOGOS uses natural language in a special way as notation; RETAIN/370 is designed for users with a highly technical orientation who feel comfortable with a highly technical notation.

EXERCISE FOR STUDENTS

Write a book on the notation problem. Caution: Many have shattered their careers on these rocky shores.

TRUTH IS HOW YOU KNOW YOU'RE DONE

Machines use signs denotatively, but it must be clearly understood that all they can denote is other signs. The machine can point to another address in memory, but it cannot point out into the world. The machine does not have access to the meaning of the symbols in the same sense that a clock does not have access to time. People have access to meaning. In a human/machine ensemble, the machine will be cut off from meanings but the ensemble will not.

Of course, people are already inextricably involved in computer systems at all levels. To say that people must become more involved in computer performance means that the degree, extent, and locus of the human involvement which already exists must be made more manifest, more flexible, and closer to the end user.

Let us consider the clock, the prototypical modern automatic machine. It is designed, built, and used. Only the designer need understand anything about how time is measured—the clock's function. The builder need know nothing about time, and the user may simply take it for granted that time is something it's useful to keep track of. The completed clock is autonomous, requiring only occasional attention from user or repair person.

Computers hark back to an older notion of machine.

> Machine 1. A structure of any kind, material or immaterial; a fabric, an erection.
>
> *Oxford English Dictionary*

The computer is a machine whose structure—material and immaterial—encompasses designer, programmer, and user, as well as hardware and software. Understanding of the nature of its function is presumed (frequently gratuitously) at all three levels; moreover, aspects of the understanding of all three—designer, programmer, and user—contribute to (or limit) the power of the machine.

Or think of the computer as an instrument that embodies the notions of both speculative instrument (as defined by I. A. Richards) and musical instrument. This metaphor illuminates the significance of the people involved at all levels. Computer use bears an interesting resemblance to piano playing, in which knowledge of music is presumed at all three levels (builder, composer, and pianist) and in which the individuals at all three levels contribute to the final character of a performance—the craftsmanship of the builder, the adeptness at expression of the composer, and the virtuosity of the performer. Furthermore, we observe in the case of music that some degree of shared vocabulary is evident in the various disciplines which contribute to a performance.

Some sense of shared responsibility for the end result has not yet evolved in the computing transmit. Between programmers and engineers there is very little in the way of shared vocabulary or technique, and users often think of themselves as merely users—they think that someone else designed the machine. In fact, almost all users redesign the machine; they are simply not aware that that is what they are doing, and so they do not follow sound design procedures. If the word "machine" is understood in the broader sense mentioned above—that is, to include software and people as well as hardware—the relationship of the user to the system is more clearly revealed. The user must see that he or she is a part of the fabric that makes up the machine and that the material-immaterial structure includes the unique capabilities of the human brain.

It is well at this point to distinguish between "access" and "virtuosity." Machines will be made accessible to everyone, just as music is accessible to everyone in the sense that anyone can learn "Chopsticks." But there is no reason to believe that sound achievement or true virtuosity will become any more common in computer use than in music. They are difficult and take practice, and not everyone can get to Carnegie Hall.

Machine design will serve as an index of legitimate authority in many fields, a test of completion of apprenticeship, and the hallmark of a master in most well-organized disciplines. It is further probable that human/program/goal systems for complex applications will manifest themselves as human/human/program/goal systems, where the second human will be the true virtuoso on the machine. Human/program/goal, the kernel of human/human/program/goal, has already been explored to some degree in on-line application programming, notably with APL and BASIC. However, these pioneering efforts have three significant limitations which must be lifted for a broader applicability of human/program/goal:

1. The user writes a "program," which is hard.
2. This program can only reflect the formalizable aspect of things.
3. Storage is prestructured.

Given the choice, most people would prefer not to program. Computers should program, and some people should help them. Software cannot continue to be built as it is today; it must be built by other software and designed by users. The path from design to production must be fully automated.

We need programs which will allow a number of people to pursue a goal without having to write a "program" first, allow nonalgorithmic solutions with human interaction built in, and permit access to storage that is free from preconceptions.

The fact that we can currently reflect only the formalizable aspects is the stickler. Most machines are lockstepped into discrete formal operation. Dreyfus despaired of ever developing machine receptors which could do outboard discrimination and process context-dependent information. Perhaps new technology (miniaturization and associative processing) and a better understanding of how this process works in humans will reduce the barrier. But for machines ever to replace humans completely would require, as Dreyfus recognized, that the machines be given extensive analog capability, and analog computing continues to lag behind at the plugboard stage. Although it is true that the new digital machines on the horizon are orders of magnitude more powerful, which will mean some reduction of these barriers, just because a barrier is reduced does not mean that it will go away entirely. It only suggests that the balance of human/machine contribution to problem solving will shift, giving over more tasks to the machines as their capacity increases and our understanding of processes allows us to identify greater areas for formalization. The human may always be required; in fact, more and better formalization will free humans to explore their unique contribution more fully.

One possible solution is a machine architecture with some sort of metaphor processor attached to the store instead of an ALU. Another is truly integrated human/machine architecture such that part of a program may read:

. . .
machine instruction
machine instruction
machine instruction
human decision
machine instruction
machine instruction
. . .

To extend our computer-as-instrument metaphor, programming packages should be considered as nickelodeon rolls which play an instrument that will in fact admit of more diversified use. (Early programs were, of course, just that: first barrel organ cylinders, later looms.)

A pianist may improvise at a piano or run a nickelodeon roll, but more likely he or she will play from sheet music (or memory thereof). This last aspect of computer use has been largely ignored, but it makes eminent sense. On-line data entry and retrieval protocols have just begun to explore this possibility, but to date they have been unimaginative, with the sheet music resembling business forms and the interpretation allowed almost negligible. When these techniques come into their own, programming will take on the character it has when hobbyists do it: designing programs to get results rather than for generality, to last, and so on. What will last is the architecture which allows this activity.

Many workers before Dreyfus recognized the limitations of digital machines. Shannon, who was particularly aware of the difference between human and digital computer architecture, suggested human/machine systems to solve problems which neither could solve alone. Indeed, the best systems today—maintenance information, insurance fraud, and so on—are human/machine partnerships. The formal manipulation of nonformal notions will increase using present technology, but we also must learn to use the nonformal notions in control. The best way to do this currently is with a human in the loop, built right into the architecture.

EARLY GREEK ORAL PROPAGANDA

The work of Cora and John Sowa in computer-implemented content analysis is an interesting example of the formal manipulation of nonformal notions. Propaganda analysis is a method of examining the changing bias of a writer of propaganda by locating and analyzing words that are commonly conjoined. Combining this technique with those of computerized document-retrieval systems, the Sowas studied the Homeric hymns of early Greek oral poetry.[4] They were interested in the development in these poems of traditional themes (withdrawal and return of the hero, marriage of the fertility goddess, etc.) as manifested by the frequency of use of common clusters of words. Because this poetry was composed orally, they believed that location and analysis of such clusters would also provide insight into the processes of word association going on in the poet's mind at the time of composition.[5]

The Sowas' characterization of their clumping algorithm is very suggestive:

> Suppose we imagine the set of all stems in the text as a complex web of interconnections. Each stem would represent one node in the network. If two stems never occurred in the same context, there would be no direct connection between them. Two stems that occurred together frequently would be connected by a strong cord, and two stems that occurred in the same context only once or twice would be connected by a weak thread.[6]

The clump program in effect builds a network, then tears it apart, threads breaking but cords holding.

The Sowas indicate that intuition may as easily mislead as

guide. They note that some meaning is lost when an intuitive notion (like association) is translated into a mathematical formula. If the formula "incorporates real insight into the structure of the problem, however, it may turn out to be more useful than the original intuitive notion."[7]

As they developed the program, the Sowas tried out a number of variations on the standard version, including varying the definition of context in which clustered stems would be looked for, varying the formulas for defining the connection between two stems, and varying the formulas for defining clusters. They note that the "usual way of minimizing a function by trial and error is to start with a good guess and then to refine the guess by making small changes. . . ."[8] Using a computer to help refine the guesses reduces the time required and is an excellent example of how human and machine can complement each other in problem solving.

In addition, the Sowas point out that the computer output did not represent a finished interpretation; some of the groups of words furnished were relevant to their study, and some were not. The value of involving the computer in the study was that it served as a counting and remembering device to assist them in keeping in mind the thousands of word forms and stems which formed the associations being studied. "There are too many words and too many relationships to grasp and remember all at once."[9]

The Sowas conclude that the importance of their work lies in the fact that they "are developing a tool which can be used to study literature of any language, oral or literate."[10] They have also developed techniques which begin to facilitate a language between human and machine. Consider: The Sowas and the computer both understand Greek better than the Sowas understand PL/I or the computer understands English. Ancient Greek word stems, then, have served as a human-computer communication vehicle which is syntax- and semantic-free, and the Sowas have turned ancient Greek to the very modern purpose of investigating thought by machine. The important point is that they and their program can use the frequency of Greek word stems to investigate anything that is written about in Greek. In this sense, Greek is a human/machine language in their investigation.

Imagine that you are given three subroutines. The first subroutine, when past an address, will return a 0 if the location pointed to contains a thing, and a 1 if it does not. The second subroutine, when past the address of a thing and a second address, will return a 0 if the second address points to an essential property of the thing, and a 1 if it points to an accidental property. The third subroutine, when past two addresses, will return a 0 if the two entities pointed to bear a family resemblance to each other, and a 1 if they do not. Calling this package from your own pseudolanguage, you could write a program which would solve one of the current outstanding problems in programming, such as reading Kanji.

It should be clear that we can provide such a subroutine package if we use the Von Kempelen ploy. We merely hook up a person to a terminal, and when the subroutine package is called, we query our living, breathing person and get an opinion.

INFORMATION AND CONTROL

Toulmin observes that Weiner's lasting contribution to science is that his mathematics ignores the mind-body distinction which shackled science for 200 years.[11] Ignoring the distinction between machine and user will have a similar liberating effect. Information and control will collapse into each other.

We know how information and control work on one macro level: through the process of learning. It is a common practice among parents, in order to keep their children from being run over by a truck, to program them to be controlled by some information so that there is some program/information combination which will result almost certainly in the child's stopping on command. However, for most levels, information and control do not have the tidy learning metaphor to bind them. How does a newt grow a new arm?

Programmed control requires three features:

1. A program
2. Control parameters
3. Some machine for the program to assimilate the control parameters with

Much linguistic evidence has been mustered to support the belief that there is a basic opposition in thought between me and not-me, between One and Two. A proper feeling for the emergence of not-one may lead to a better understanding of information and control. The line between a person and that person's hammer is pretty clear-cut, but the distinction between an individual and that individual's knowledge is less easily drawn. In the area where human and information interact, control of human over information and vice versa is expressed.

METAPHYSICAL EXERCISE FOR STUDENTS

Go into the machine room and look at the ALU (if you can find it; if not, just look at the tape drives). Think: "Wherein not me?"

The difference between information and control is that information is when searching stops and acting begins. An example: In teleprocessing, we distinguish between data and control (device control, link control, or path control), but data itself eventually becomes control, as when an "A" translates into tilt/rotate code on the Selectric. What is printed by the Selectric is data until some human perceives some information in the printout. All is initially data; as the data moves through the system, various bits cause action and are stripped off, until finally at the Selectric all bits left are interpreted as tilt/rotate and an "A" is printed (and a new system has been entered and an analogous process starts in the person reading the "A").

Because we wish to impart control, a new dimension is added to the usual problem of analog-to-digital conversion. (The usual problem is: Will the approximation serve the purpose?) A discrete system can only approximate a continuous system, but a continuous system can exactly emulate a digital system, and so there is a great danger of the machines swinging us over to their way of thinking. The power of formal systems over human thought has gone too far already without having this trend accelerated by machines. Perhaps the new Luddites sense this, and insofar as we are unable to circumvent the problem, perhaps they are right.

Consider an analogy between human/machine boundary crossings and hardware boundary crossings. Transfer of information between systems with a possible control corollary is called "boundary crossing," and in engineering terms each boundary crossing represents a cost. Methods are constantly being devised for reducing the cost of crossing hardware boundaries. In human/machine systems these devised methods relate to the cost of computing components only, sometimes at the expense of the human or the program. The human costs of boundary crossing, when information and control are transferring, are more difficult to assess. This problem has not been adequately investigated because engineers have not seen fit to take up psychology and psychologists are pretty inept at engineering. What has been done in this field goes loosely under the rubric of "human factors"—people get frustrated (a human cost) if they have to wait more than 2 seconds, people get spooky if equipment is too quiet, and so forth.

Whatever the boundary-crossing costs are to a human/machine system, the system, being adaptive, will move to reduce them. A problem arises here, and it is serious; it could be called the "TV problem." In the case of human/television interaction, the human is the more adaptive partner, and so there is a tendency for the human to adapt to the TV (watch whatever is on) rather than for the TV to adapt to the human (programming changes), which involves a long and complex feedback loop. The same problem arises in a human/program-in-computing-machine partnership. The human can adapt quickly, but the feedback for the machine to adapt (particularly if the human is not a programmer) is long and complex.

What is on television is due largely to accidents of history and the subsequent skewing of evolution by considerations of the marketplace. Current human/machine systems are also early accidents, and the systems of the future will evolve from them. We should tamper with existing systems in the direction of incorporating more sophisticated assumptions than are found in the average bit of FORTRAN so that the systems of the future will have evolved from happier accidents. As a minimum step toward this goal, the feedback loop for machine adaptation must be shortened so that machines will be at least as adaptable as humans—a tall order. Otherwise, the machines will win out as we adapt to them. It will not be an exotic win of the sci-fi type, but a win of drudgery, inconsequence, boredom, and stacks of output.

EDUCATE US, TRAIN THEM

There is an important distinction between education and training: Education involves assimilating general principles, while training involves acquiring specific skills. Insofar as this distinction holds up, should we expect to educate a program or train it? In what sense do we want a program to learn? We want the program to acquire something which it previously did not have, but we do not want it to use this to speculate about metaphysics or ethics. However, we do wish for the program to perform beyond mere imitation, and so we want to train programs.

Training and education frequently go hand in hand. Weinberg notes that training in Job Control Language is essential before any education in the principles of operating systems can take place. Similarly, training in reading is a prerequisite to education in most other fields. When we think of changing the behavior of a human/machine system (that is, training and eduction), we should address the system as an ensemble. Programs will respond best to training, humans to education. One result will be that many trainable tasks can be unloaded onto programs.

We know that in some sense a program can learn. Briefly, the approach is to develop a strategy which aims to minimize the expectation of penalty. To develop such a strategy in terms of Shannon's analysis requires that it be based on well-formulated questions; that is, a question must have an identifiable set of possible answers to each of which we may assign an improbability. People (as opposed to machines) continually develop strategies for random environments without the requirement that the range of possible questions about the environment be well formulated.

Compared to a person, the automaton is at a severe disadvantage, for formulating the question is usually by far the most difficult task. Questions are formulated for automata by people. The way this is done now is that programmers usually formulate which questions a program will ask. Frequently, they do not consider the ramifications of what they are doing (indeed, they frequently do not even understand the ultimate goals of the program they are writing). Users should be able to formulate which questions the program asks while they are using the program.

ASSUMPTION SPACE

In a human/human/program system, certain tasks will fall naturally to the program, others naturally to the human; this division of labor will shift through mutual adaptation and education. Homogeneous data space and more informal access to instruction space will facilitate the shift. Assumption space (the place where assumptions are) currently includes both data and instructions.

At first, it might seem that assumptions are a purely human domain. The user is presumed to know what he or she is trying to do, any goals are certainly couched in terms of the user's presuppositions, and any assumptions embedded in the machine were put there by humans. But the assumptions we bring to any undertaking are so subtle, deeply entrenched, and pervasive that we sometimes are not aware of them. The assumptions of the designer and the programmer, as well as the user, influence the outcome of any computer performance, as we have pointed out. Thus, it would seem wise to have some outside force shaking the assumption tree. Genius frequently has this effect, but since we do not know how genius works, we cannot incorporate it into our system (except by including a real live genius).

FIVE

MODELS OF REALITY

A model is a set of symbols with an assigned system of relationships; it represents some interpretation or theory about reality by close analogy. A model, then, is a formal kind of metaphor. This interpretation rests on the assumption that the reality represented is systematic. There are two troublesome notions in this characterization of a model: "set" and "assigned."

As Ziff has pointed out, natural language may not constitute a "set" in the sense of set theory, which results in the first discrepancy between any theory and its corresponding model: No matter how chaste the entities and stringent the relations of a theory, they cannot escape being stated in language and hence defying precise correspondence with any set of symbols and relations which may constitute a model.[1]

The importance of "assigned" is that a model will remain based on the relationships assigned to it. Everything changes except the relationships assigned to a model. As the world turns and our understanding of it grows, the relationships assigned to a model do not change. Moreover, there is a singular poverty of available relationships which can be assigned to a computer model; they are all computational relationships. We could do a better job modeling reality if we developed a human interface to the model which would allow the assigned relationships of the model to reside in the user, not in the model. In other words, the assigned relationships of a model should be in data space, not instruction space, and the data space should include the mind of the user.

Modeling is attractive because it provides a means of obtaining information indirectly about the modeled reality. (When direct methods are available, use them.) The information may be descriptive, as was the case with Watson and Crick's model of the DNA molecule. It may be used to understand better the workings of some system in order to improve its function—for example, traffic patterns in a metropolitan area. It may be used to predict such things as profit margin or plant requirements when a large corporation tries to do long-range planning. The possibilities for productive use are enormous but are currently limited. New tools for modeling are needed because the old tools cannot portray the complexity of reality called for by modern enterprises.

To begin with, the limitations of the available notation result in special problems for models as information. We seem somehow to be restricted in our vision of the possibilities by the one-dimensional linear quality of writing on paper. Wind tunnels and models of molecules (like Watson and Crick's DNA model, built out of wire and pieces of tin) are happy exceptions. But such physical analogs are often not practical or even possible, and we are confined to pencil and paper, a near relative of cave painting. Such limitations are no longer necessary, and an examination of new possibilities (such as holography) is just beginning.

In addition, computer models restrict the available set of assigned system relationships too severely. Because we have as yet no general method of representing or processing aspects of reality which cannot be stated in formal terms in a computer, simplification is used, with attendant loss of power. In part this is a programming problem and has several aspects: how programming is done and by whom, and the kinds of functions that can be programmed into a model.

Despite these limitations, the advent of computers has started an epidemic of modeling; in fact, computer models have become a hallmark of respectability like the tower clock of medieval times. Let's take a look at some of the problems as they turn up in modeling projects.

THE GREAT ELECTRONIC HOPE: MODELING FOR MANAGEMENT

John Kemeny noted in *Man and the Computer* (New York, Scribner's, 1972) that the needs of top management of any large institution would be well served by a computer model of how the institution functions.[2] An effective model of operations requires projection into the future, and the problem here is one that has bothered humankind for more than 2500 years: Truths about the future are not like truths about the past. Projection is not factual, and so we must use principles. Suppose some automobile-manufacturing executives are attempting to plan for the future. Can battery-powered electric cars be made acceptable to the car-buying public? Their concern is with the potential customers, not the relevant technology. The question has a potentially great impact on their business.

Now obviously:

1. The executives are not interested in the theory of the truth of propositions.
2. The question is in some sense answerable, in that there is no reason in principle why a rational course of action cannot be arrived at.
3. Intuition will likely provide important guidance, and machines currently offer little help in channeling intuition.

The question will be best answered through integrating educated guesses with careful calculation. Computers can and should be designed to be very helpful in educating the guess.

Kemeny would like to have a model with lots of variables and formulas, which corresponds to the operation of Dartmouth College. That is a big job. Kemeny might even consider the Equity Funding ploy: Close school and just run the model. But to get what he really wants—a model which will help him project his plans into the murky future—he will have to rethink the workings of human/program/goal, ask himself just wherein Nature is lawful, and resolve, at least at some working level, the questions of information and control.

Kemeny thinks that with modeling, management can anticipate disaster rather than wait for it to occur. He has in mind, apparently, events like a hurricane, which, if we knew enough about meteorology, we could at least predict and perhaps control. (If we reserve the word "disaster" for those discontinuities which cannot be predicted, then obviously the local laws of nature do not meet the modeling task.)

A note on costs: It would probably be cheaper to play it by ear, for Dartmouth College. But the technology must be developed somewhere, and it seems for some reason that systems will be built whether or not they make any sense economically. Modeling has made great strides in the social sciences where worthless results are very difficult to detect.

EXERCISE FOR STUDENTS

Would a model of your commune's operating structure really give you any useful information about the consequences of the addition of a new member (besides predicting such disasters as a bed shortage)?

Any large organization, such as a business or university, is a machine in the old sense ("structure, fabric, erection"). Attempts to model such a structure, though increasingly common, have many hazards. Stamper warns that the use of mathematical formulations can deceive us into believing that we have separated the denotative from the affective. He states that a "mathematical formulation of an organisational problem will yield its quota of dubious value-judgments lurking in the supposedly objective choice of variables and equations."[3]

It is our opinion that at the current state of the art, imparting the essence of "cat" to a machine is beyond the capability of even the most able programmer and most knowledgeable biologist. If even this basic level of ostensive definition eludes us, is it any wonder that we end up in ritualistic use of mathematical models, that is, not only playing games but playing them for their own sake? "Space War" is a model rightly enjoyed for its own sake; real war is a game which should not be enjoyed for its own sake, yet the Pentagon has the models which would allow one to do so. Equity Funding played "Life Insurance" for fun and profit. (The real significance of the cashless society is this: Money is merely a medium of information, and it is considered by some to be outdated because it is too slow. Equity Funding caught on to this early and made a few dollars. The basic elements of wealth will remain the same; it is the information system used to exchange wealth which is undergoing overhaul. Information about all this will be exchanged at the speed of light rather than the speed of currency. Money, after all, was originally introduced for mobility, not speed.)

At first blush, then, it would seem easier to program more abstract concepts, such as "projected profit," than more concrete concepts, such as "cat." Actually, it is even harder (note that many companies have gone bankrupt with abstract profits). What is easy to program are empty or meaningless concepts. These have their uses, one supposes, but there is great danger in confusing them with their better-founded counterparts.

In addition, there is the danger of trying to make the organization run like the model instead of making the model model the organization. "We must exercise caution when trying to extend a design process appropriate for the development of machinery into the sphere of organisational design."[4] The specs on the components are unreliable because we do not (or will not) understand human nature and in particular human communication protocols. Most system analysis is in fact projective rather than retrospective, and a lot of gross assumptions are made about what people can be made to do. These assumptions frequently prove faulty, and so the system fails.

THE INVISIBLE HAND, HAVING WRIT, MOVES ON. TRY TO MODEL THAT.

The market economy (or invisible hand) nowadays operates efficiently only in specialized or localized situations. The black market, illegal drug market, and certain agricultural markets still function well when left alone. But most markets are now administered, and this is true in capitalist as well as socialist countries. In most markets, the decision makers in the large organizations are isolated from the marketplace. Now administrators, like bureaucrats, rarely feel the tug of the old *quid pro quo*. What was the invisible hand doing? Passing around information at the local level.

In general, it doesn't work anymore. One aim of the information theorist is to create a visible hand to regulate the designed environment, much as the invisible hand regulated the natural environment. (Great social dangers attend the visible hand; the potential iniquity attendant to the abuse of centralized information dwarfs the inequities of the invisible hand.)

EXERCISE FOR STUDENTS

Entrust yourself to the invisible hand. You will note that first information is exchanged, then goods or services. In barter-

ing, you will discover anew all the things to which economists give fancy names: how badly you want whatever; how much of whatever is around; if you are bartering with something you have made, what the value of your work is; and so on. To do this, go to a rock festival and barter throughout. Afterwards you will have a lot of information: Weed is a little scarce, too many people are making candles, there seems to be a swing back to alcohol, there is never enough ice, the ratio of available women to available men is actually rising after all these years, you have to eat to live, and so on. Now, imagine that you are a corporate officer in a large conglomerate that has holdings in petroleum (candles), South American real estate (weed), advertising (cheap wine), and textiles (sexual partners), and that also has a commodities portfolio (you have to eat to live). How might you have gotten the information to make appropriate decisions without attending the rock festival? Could you incorporate such information into a useful model? (Be careful. There are many, many pitfalls; what seems obvious with the music blaring can become nearly opaque at corporate headquarters.)

THE CONTINUUM IN THE COMPUTER ROOM, OR, THE PROBLEM WITH FORMAL MODELS

In a human/machine system, the user can provide directly the functions which map information around the store. However, there is a problem. The machine can host language so that parameters may easily pass from the human, but how is a discrete machine to manipulate language other than by formal algorithm programmed in? How is information from the continuous human system to control the discrete machine system? For something essential is changed in analog-to-digital conversion, as surely as when the future flows into the past.

Consider an informal mapping like an analogy. Say we wish to investigate the assertion that marketing some new type of product will closely resemble marketing some product in the past. In a machine-aided investigation, we would want the computer to handle analogy with the same agility with which it now handles deduction. Yet aside from statistics, we currently do not know how to program the looser forms of inference, and although we can certainly get the computer to host an analogy, we cannot yet contrive to get it to manipulate its data space with an analogy. The problem can be seen as one of translating function from data space to instruction space.

Probably the most dangerous problem with formal models is that they tend to pull us to them and force us to adapt. Little effort has been dedicated toward redesigning the machines to make them more flexible, but a lot of subtle pressure exists to push people toward conforming to the machines. Commenting on Minsky and other students of artificial intelligence and cognitive simulation, Dreyfus observes that they are operating under the assumption that "human behavior must be formalizable in terms of a heuristic program for a digital computer."[5] In other words, for workers in artificial intelligence, the computer itself has become a working metaphor descriptive of human thought. This assumption of formalizableness must somehow be put to rest if there is to be significant progress in this use of computer models.

There is a strong possibility that if the power of the computer metaphor increases unchecked in our society, its impact will have the effect of encouraging us to model our behavior more closely on that of computers. We may thereby become formalizable because we believe we are. This is a very real danger; and if we are to think our way outside of this box, now is the time to do so because the walls of the box are being reinforced daily as bigger and bigger computers are put in place and set to running under formal assumptions. What is needed both to avoid this dreary prospect and to increase the usefulness of computers is to go beyond formalist assumptions, seductive in part because of their compatability with the computer's architecture, and learn instead how to reflect the richer, nonformalizable spectrum of human thought in our machines.

Here is a good example of the wrong kind of thinking: In an interview published in *Computer world,* Professor G. Popov of the Institute of Cybernetics at Kiev says: "Decision-making is the prerogative of the human being."[6] So far, so good. He adds that it will be from 10 to 15 years before the computer will be sufficiently sophisticated to be capable of performing medical diagnostics. But Popov believes that even if such machines were available now, we would be unable to use them to their full potential:

> POPOV: They would simply go to waste as the doctors are not yet prepared to handle them. The doctors cannot think the way computers are accustomed to "thinking." They cannot communicate with the computers. What does "communicating with the computer" mean? Above all it means being able to express oneself with precision and in no uncertain terms. However, if doctoring is an art then the terms it uses are most ambiguous, as is the case with any art. Take, for instance, myocardial infarction which has dozens of nuances for which we have no names so far. How can we carry on a dialog with the computer? The most important thing now, therefore, is to do preparatory work.
>
> INTERVIEWER: In other words, you want to *get doctors to think in a computer-like fashion* before the computers are available? (Emphasis ours.)
>
> POPOV: Precisely.

Precisely not, Popov. The question is, Do we want doctors who think like computers or computers who think like doctors, or if not like them, at least with them? Popov's future will come about only if computers continue to think in the manner in which they are "accustomed" to thinking. Popov takes this as given, but it is not necessarily so.

MODELING WHOLE SYSTEMS IN SCIENCE

We envision the following interchange between a program and an investigator some time in the future:

S?

Y

The program has asked, S?: Am I to assume synergy is the case, i.e., that macrosystems manifest properties which cannot be reduced to the properties of their components? The investigator has answered, *Y:* Yes. This is a hot issue in many areas. For example, in anthropology, is society merely a sum of social relations, or is there a deep underlying reality of which the relations can be considered aspects? Similarly for biology: Can the laws of biology ultimately be reduced to the laws of physics and chemistry, or is the whole greater than the sum of its parts? Similarly for linguistics: Can the entire meaning of a sentence be explicated in terms of its constituent morphemes? And architecture: Does a tetrahedron have properties not implied by the properties of triangles? And art criticism, and human psychology, and so on. And human/machine systems: Do they (or will they) have properties which cannot be reduced to properties of their constituents?

The view that an organism should be investigated as a whole system rather than reduced to its physical and chemical components is called "holism." Despite obvious suitability to the study of living things, the approach presents some serious problems for experimental design. Holism has methodological problems, and its far-reaching implications cannot be easily stated; furthermore, the notation problem is particularly intractable.[7]

To expand on this a little, the study of a whole biological system (e.g., an animal or the nervous system) presents three problems not encountered in investigations conducted at a more "atomistic" level (e.g., biochemical or molecular studies).

The first problem is projection. Although it is easy to state holistic theories, it is difficult to design experiments to test them. This is because the projective inferences are not deductive. By comparison, formal systems give the illusion of projection because of the number of tautological truths that they can be permuted into. Actually, these are not projections in any sense other than that they display a snapshot of the implications of a body of assumptions.

Then there is the problem of method. Measurement has supplied a methodology for reductionist investigation which has no parallel at the level of whole organisms. The apparent rigor of measurement is actually misleading, but it does render up numbers, which are nice discrete entities. No readily measurable features of whole system lawfulness present themselves, and we are saddled with unwieldy analogs rather than nice discrete entities.

Finally, there is the problem of notation. It happens that marks on paper provide a handy notation that is isomorphic to reductionist theories. No such notation is yet available for a holistic approach; attempts to adapt notation from systems theory (boxes, arrows, or whatnot) have not been productive and introduce more confusion than they resolve.

Reductionist thinking is amenable to formalism and resolves the problems that go along with the holistic approach: It has the method of measurement, it provides at least the illusion of projection with deductions, and for notation it finds a convenient analog in marks on paper. In a formal system, the cascade of tautological truths gives an appearance of projection because these truths may at least in principle be tested in the future. Using less-rigorous forms of inference, there is no reason why a program could not similarly produce all the implications of, say, a certain analogy to be compared against available experience and the future. Measurement is itself a form of comparison, a special case in which numbers which can be plugged into formulas are rendered up. Comparison is a valuable explanatory tool, and in a human/machine system it can be broadly applied without requiring numerical readout. Model building with human/machine systems should provide a means for working out the implications of scientific lawfulness at a holistic level.

GENERAL SYSTEMS THEORY

General systems theory is an attempt to combine the study of whole systems with a mathematically formalized approach. George J. Klir, editor of *Trends in General Systems Theory* (New York, Wiley-Interscience, 1972), contrasts the systems approach—"the study of systems with strong . . . interactions between their components, as well as between each system and its environment"—with classical Newtonian methods, "which regarded an object of scientific investigation as a collection of isolated parts and tried to derive the properties of the whole object directly from the properties of its parts without considering possible interactions between the parts."[8]

Systems theory is really one huge analogy—"more and more evidence has been found that certain properties of systems do not depend on the specific nature of the individual system"[9]—and can be seen in this sense as an attempt to formalize inference patterns which are essentially unformalizable.

The paradigm case for general systems theorists occurs when the equations of one system are found to be applicable to another system, most notably when the equations of certain electrical circuits may be applied to other mechanical, acoustical, and thermal circuits. A general systems theory is not a theory in the formal sense. That is, a so-called "homomorphic" model is just a fancy analogy: "At present, there is a general trend to formalize so as to diminish conceptual confusion. As a rule, however, the process of formalization narrows the original meaning of the entities concerned."[10] Klir is saying that the more precisely we define our terms, the less homomorphic our models become, resulting in the impoverishment of fully formalized concepts.

Klir would like to preserve the semantically rich concepts of systems theory, but because he does not know how to defend them from the onslaught of the formalists, he opts for allowing various formal schemes to account for aspects of his semantically rich concepts. Connotationless language (plus deductive logic) is the essence of formalization, and semantic richness can mean nothing other than lots of connotations.

In addition to clearing out semantic richness, simplification is required to make computation manageable, and we now have a rough handle on what the practical computational powers of a digital computer are (give or take 10^{10}). The known upper bound on the feasibility of digital computations gives systems theorists confidence when they talk about complexity. They feel that although the actual complexity of a given system may not be known, the subset of that complexity which we may usefully compute is known roughly. Thus, to compute we must simplify.

Clearly, there are other reasons for simplifying. However, we are inclined to agree with Weinberg in his discussion of Newton (in Klir's book) that the power of Newton's simplifications over people's minds was in large part due to the extent of computation (then done by humans) that they permitted.[11] Newton was able to simplify his equations because of the great relative mass of the sun compared to the mass of the other bodies in the solar system. Weinberg states that the simplification was made possible by the solar system, not by mechanics.[12] He feels no inclination to the view that this simplification was made possible by Newton, and he thus reveals himself to be free, like most Americans, of the epistemological and metaphysical burdens of Continental thinkers. In fact, *Structuralism* minus *Metaphysics* plus *Computers* is a fair characterization of systems science.

We ourselves are reluctant to whiz right by the epistemological questions without so much as a how-do-you-do, but we are inclined to find a certain charm in the American approach: It gets things done. (Not all to its credit, however, as witness the impossible turmoil the systems people created at the Pentagon. One can see in retrospect that MacNamara's whiz kids ignored for simplicity such things as an admiral's strong allegiance to the Navy, and not, one assumes, to make computation easier, but to make computation feasible, and not because of the limits of digital machines either, but because allegiance is hard to quantify.)

Here is Weinberg's view of what general systems theory is: "It is his [the general systems theorist's] chosen task to understand the simplifying assumptions of science—those assumptions which delimit its field of application and magnify its power of predictions."[13] This is supposed to help the general systems theorist in suggesting useful models for other sciences, with the result that the progress of human knowledge is less dependent on a genius like Newton. But all this is geared to one mode of understanding: computational. In fact, as a general rule, you can assume that people who bring up Newton are fixing to take this tack.

The success of classical mechanics in particular and what are known as the "hard" sciences in general is frequently given as the reason for taking up these subjects or their methods. Their success has clear material and materialistic manifestations, such as space travel. But, entailing as it did a complete reorganization of humanity's conception of itself, hasn't the impact of Darwin's thinking been at least as great? Darwin, too, simplified, and no one can question that his generalizations are elegant. But it seems inappropriate to argue that he was either motivated by the search for or achieved computational manageability.

Something, we feel certain, will supersede formalism as the species continues to adapt. It may be the flint tools of 300,000 years ago, but more likely when general systems theory comes to an end, not with a bang but the whimper of a multitrillion-byte memory glut, then some other strategy for the useful application of digital storage to the study of whole systems will emerge. New goals will be set for the science of systems, and new variations will have a chance to try their stretch to close the gap between the new goals and the degree to which humans perceive themselves to fall short of them. Here are some suggestions on how to proceed:

1. Identify and legitimatize new goals.
2. Examine extant variations.
3. Study the historical processes through which populations develop, and attempt to engender a fruitful atmosphere for adaptive evolution.

PRACTICAL EXERCISE FOR STUDENTS

Become a variation in the profession. Do not overlook the necessity to develop in a niche.

OPENING THE SYSTEMS

A human and a computer program pursuing a goal, with information passing back and forth between the human and the program, is a system. (It goes without saying that the human needs a body and the computer program needs a computer. When we say "computer," we assume that it has a program in it; when we say "program," we assume that it has a computer around it. The distinction between hardware and software is nonessential.)

Such a system (human and program) uses a computer as a tool to increase the range and facility with which we may apply what I. A. Richards calls "speculative instruments"—any theory, definition, algorithm, or concept used to expand knowledge or heighten awareness.[14] Speculative instruments are analogous to such other instruments as the microscope and the spectrometer. In the case of these more concrete instruments, however, we remain aware of the need to keep them in good repair and be ever conscious of their limitations and possible biases. Richards urges us to maintain a similar concern for the use of our intellectual (speculative) instruments. Theories, definitions, and concepts are tools we employ to deal with the world, understand the past, and plan for the future. Whether we call it a "history" or an "annual report," a "market projection" or a "falsifiable hypothesis," we are bringing into service some variety of speculative instrument.

The computer's ability to run rapidly through permutations holds out the possibility that if properly used, it will enable us to hone our speculative instruments more finely as well as enlarge the variety of such instruments available to us. But we must remember that computers are actually speculative instruments for using speculative instruments. Ignoring this, as we currently do, has the effect of entrenching our conceptual presuppositions ever more deeply.

Because they are more open systems, human/machine ensembles will help scientists do science at the macro level where holistic biologists, for example, wish to use the model to investigate structure, system, and function. What do we mean by a more open system? In a closed, static system, all truths are tautological except those truths which are assumed. In a closed, dynamic system, the same holds; and without input, the closed, dynamic system will loop endlessly through its truths. What we are accustomed to consider as closed systems usually have in fact open data space (such as punched card reader); we may enter and retrieve data from this open space, with intermediate processing by the instruction space. Our results are tautological and the process is formal, which makes the use of such systems particularly amenable to the formalizable parts of a process: comparison, computation, and so on.

When our tautologies prove to be anomalies, we need a programmer to debug our instruction space. We stop our dynamic system, fool with one of its static states, and then start it up again. Since there has as yet emerged no generally usable formal check on the procedure for building the system, we are forever debugging in this fashion. Thus closed systems usually do have open data space and, for a programmer, sort of open instruction space. Why, then, do we call them "closed"? Because their *assumption space* is inaccessible: relatively so when the assumptions are embedded in the instruction space, absolutely so when the assumptions are embedded in the architecture of the machine which hosts the system. (Remember: *Assumptions exist, and their domain is assumption space.*)

These architectural assumptions are well hidden, deeply embedded, and when exhumed, usually the sorts of things that everyone would take for granted at first glance. For example, every proposition is true or false. Well it so happens that in a closed system every proposition *is* true or false but only in the sense that it is or is not a tautology. This confusion feeds on itself, and people generally are inclined to leave it there. Another assumption frequently found in assumption space is that such and such a process is linear. Now we know that in nature almost nothing is linear, yet people are still inclined to leave this assumption intact, too.

EXERCISE FOR CLASSICAL STUDENTS

Computation has an inherent flaw. To convince yourself of this, write a program on the assumption that an arrow shot from a bow must reach the midway point before it reaches the target. (Of course, before it reaches this midway point, it must reach the midway point between it and the bow, and so on.) If the arrow's "muzzle velocity" is 107 miles per hour and the target is 100 yards away, how long will it take to get there? (Hint: It never gets there.)

THINKING ABOUT REALITY

Formal, deductive logic is one of the conceptual models we use to think about reality. It is a valuable tool of science, but it is not an immutable constituent of the cosmos; that is, "*p* is not not-*p*" is an epistemological construct, not an ontological primitive. Consider the statement "Electricity is like water," a useful statement in training electricians. Suppose we wish to assess the statment's status as an explanation. We will find that $E = W$ will produce some statements that are true, like "Electricity flows," and some that are false, like "Electricity will get you wet." But we are still nowhere near assessing $E = W$ as an explanation. In fact, this cannot be done formally; there is no formal notion of "like."

Very rarely in the normal course of events do we encounter people processing information by way of deduction. ("Hmm. Let's see. All *A* is *B* and all *B* is *C*. So . . . all *A* must be *C*!") But frequently we encounter people processing information by way of implicit analogy. ("Hmm. It worked once, and so it may work again!") Thus we might expect computers, by way of amplifying our information-processing capability, to increase our power to use analogy.

A typical argument (argument being a good prototype of rational behavior) might run as follows. "*A* is like *B*." "But *A* differs from *B* in these respects." "*A*'s likeness to *B* is not to the point in those respects." "*B* is in turn like *C* in some of those respects so that *A* may be like *C* in some ways." "No, *A* is nothing like *B* when you think about it." "Of course *A* is like *B; A is B*." "*A* is more like *D* than it is like *B*." "Most *A* is like *B*, but this *A* is the exception that proves the rule," and so on.

There are always many ways in which an analogy breaks

down; these must be identified and evaluated for relevance. But there are also always ways in which any analogy brings new insights and suggests new leads; these too must be identified and evaluated. Computers will be very helpful in the identification process because identification is largely iterative, something people aren't very good at. Evaluation is more suited to humans, but with ingenuity, some of the evaluative process may be preprogrammed and reprogrammed into the machine (reprogramming being the best method we have at present of teaching a machine). Here we find another strong indication that programming will be application-oriented because the ways in which analogy is useful differ from endeavor to endeavor. It is different, for example, for theology, law, or love.

Macrolevel explanation is not rigorous, as a cursory review of the literature will reveal, but resembles natural language explanation; that is, there is much argument by analogy, illustration, and metaphor. Rarely if ever is a formal deduction introduced. Anthropology provides a good example. The task of anthropology (especially structuralist anthropology) has been defined as the description of the life-styles of certain societies in terms of the societies themselves, as well as finding affinities between the life-styles of primitive societies and those of civilized people. Perhaps we can see how one might use a human/machine system to do things anthropologically. The key phrases in this definition are "in terms of" the society itself and "affinities."

Describing something in its own terms means that we are going to provide the person or program to whom we are describing the phenomenon sufficient information about the new subject so that he or she or it begins to get its flavor and will thus not be forced to view the new phenomenon wholly in terms of existing preconceptions.

Having gone this far, we now look for affinities between the new phenomenon and some more familiar one in order to identify similarities and differences in the hope of a better understanding of the new phenomenon. Anything with which the program or person is sufficiently familiar will serve as a model; models will be more or less useful insofar as they have strong similarities to the new phenomenon.

In this context, comparing apples to oranges would be a very good idea. If a program knew a lot about apples, to introduce the concept of "orange" we would suggest an affinity with apples and add that the juice comes homogenized and frozen in cans, that 1 million cans of it emanate yearly from Florida, and that it seems to prevent colds. Our program may ask, "Does one a day keep the doctor away?" "Does one bad orange spoil the whole barrel?" and so on, as it struggles to assimilate the new with the known. The process of looking for affinities between new phenomena and known phenomena is one at which computers, because of their ability to look for many, rapidly, should be very good. Looking for disaffinity is as important as looking for affinity.

The question is: How can a program be meaningfully set to looking about for affinities on its own? For clearly, if it can, then phenomena of a complexity now beyond the grasp of human comprehension may be examined and explained. Turing-Von Neumann programs cannot do processing at the gross macro (meaning) level. They process only bits. They could also be written to process filaments and interstices in a net of big-bit chains.

Note that these (bits, filaments, interstices) are not properties of words but rather properties of physical objects in space which may be used to store words. Meaning will always lie outside the bounds of an exact match. That is, my love is *unlike* a red, red rose precisely in the (infinite) ways in which an encoding of "love" and an encoding or "red, red rose" do not match by bit, filament, and interstice. (To get an idea of how this could work, imagine that words are not coded in storage by the letters of their spelling but, say, by the phonemes of their pronunciation.) So although we don't know what we know, we do know where what we don't know is.

User access to and control over assumption space will be the hallmark of the truly open systems we envision, useful in modeling wholes. As a system user, one wants the ability to assign any value one likes to an assertion such as "I'll send you a check tomorrow." There is no reason why current systems cannot host any value assigned. Whether and to what degree they can manipulate these values other than formally will be determined by the direction future programming takes. But clearly, that they should be able to do so is a legitimate professional goal for programming, and as Toulmin observes, *goals* minus *achievements* defines the working set of subject matter for a profession. Development of appropriate notation is the key to metaphorical modeling with a human/machine ensemble.

SIX

THE BROAD SPECTRUM OF RATIONAL BEHAVIOR

CONFRONTING FORMALISM: a^2 HAS EQUALED $b^2 + c^2$ FOR A LONG TIME

Many concepts are of such long standing and general use that they sometimes seem to be thought of as invariant, innate, or both. Examples of such concepts are cause and effect in Kant's view, subject and predicate in Chomsky's view, and kinship in Levi-Strauss's view. The idea that everything is ultimately formalizable is also such a concept. As Toulmin points out, concepts are not truly invariant but merely change very slowly. Many of these purported invariants are loosely classifiable as information-processing concepts. One result we may anticipate, then, from accelerating and amplifying human information-processing capability using digital storage is that the underlying factors which have contributed to the slow rate of change for such concepts in the past may begin to give way. No one likes change; few can willingly fling away time-honored, cherished, apparently self-evident ideas. (A friend of ours claims that he could not face life without the law of contradiction: *A* is not not-*A*. But isn't it likely that worms, who have no eyes, and flies, who have eyes structured radically differently from ours, live without this law?

For clearly, contradiction is a highly visual notion, which is not nearly so clear and distinct in the tactile, olfactory, gustatory, or auditory realms.) It is doubtful that there are any immutable ideas, but it seems to some degree inescapable that we must act as if there were. This presents a real paradox for science, a paradox which we should also expect to see amplified as computers come to enhance the information-processing capacity of humanity.

A rigid statement of formalism would be that assertions (sentences, formulas, and the like) bear a direct and simple relationship to the world and that their interrelationships conform to the rules of formal logic. A looser statement of how things are—which saves the advantages of the stronger formal statement but circumvents many of its drawbacks—would be that assertions bear an aspectual and metaphorical relationship to the world and that their interrelationships can be of many sorts, including, but by no means exclusively limited to, the rules of formal logic. In both cases our understanding of the world is a part of the world, but in the loose version an important point shines through: We stand to our understanding of the world as creators, not merely as beholders.

Fuller reminds us that humanity has been drawn to formalism in part because of the tangible quality of the engineering by-products of those fields of inquiry in which the assumption of global formal systematization has been productive, such as trips to the moon. Formalism has been a useful metaphor; no question about that. But let us not forget the quality of the human by-products of those fields of inquiry in which the assumption of global formal systematization has been of little use, such as visual art, surgery, and agriculture.

Formalism also has consonance with subtle cultural cues, which stem from saturation by formalism itself. Thus a cultural shift is required. How does a path come to be worn in the jungle? We know at least how a new path is started: by someone striking out on his or her own. A selection of more interesting metaphors, a repertory of more flexible retrieval techniques, and arguments to render our digital stores more responsive are needed. Storage manipulation in the future will be governed by the usefulness of results integrated into human adaptive behavior. Usefulness is a teleological notion which cannot be poured into formal mathematical terms, and so the proof will have to be in the pudding.

DESIGNING BY DESIGN

The more interesting metaphors and more flexible retrieval techniques will be designed, not discovered. In general, interfaces which are arbitrary but not immaterial are the ones which can be designed. "Design" is the process of delineating the interface to a system, and "interface" indicates simply where system meets nonsystem or subsystem. (Fuller defines a system as "a configuration that divides the Universe into (1) everything outside the system; (2) the system itself; (3) everything inside the system."[1]) In systems which change (and all systems do, although some do not change to a significant degree in terms of the scale on which we encounter them), understanding the principles which govern the system and understanding something about the nonsystem it is likely to encounter are important if our design is to persist through time and continue to serve the purpose for which it is intended.

In designing an interface for the discrete machine and the continuous human, it is well to remember that when construing a continuous process to be discrete (for example, reading the time off a sundial), *purpose* is the key to how we will slice our pie. Analog pie we may slice up as we like, but this is not the case with digital pie. Digital pie is of our own contrivance, while analog pie is of Nature's. We can slice Nature's as we like; we can build ours as we like. Design is at the interface, and goals (along with other constraints like cost) will determine how we design.

What exactly is design? The state of any system at time T_1 will depend on the state of that system at time T_0 and any input I_0. In simple terms, what we end up with results from what we start with and what happens to it. Consider as a system a piece of flint lying on the ground and its surroundings. Systems tend to equilibrium; as the piece of flint lies on the ground, it will probably change only very slowly. With inputs of gentle breezes, spring rain, and falling autumn leaves, the state of the flint at T_{n+1} will be about the same as at T_n.

The odds are greatly in favor of the flint just lying there changing very slowly. However, a certain input with a probability of, for example, 10^{-50} will result in its chipping—a mastodon may step on it just so. Suppose it does chip and some hunter notices that this exposes a useful cutting edge. The hunter then undertakes to duplicate the improbable input so as to obtain a similar useful cutting edge on another piece of flint. With a human in the picture, the probabilities of various inputs change rapidly. Changing the course of a stream is controlling input in the same way, as is penning in animals to use for food or weeding unwanted plants from edible ones. Conceiving useful equifinal states through controlled input, then, is the process of design.

In computer jargon, every final state is manifested as output. Software designs control I to get useful O. Science undertakes to characterize systems so that a designer has more to go on than trial and error when controlling I. Scientists who think that science should be the search for reductionist unification of all knowledge to mathematical lawfulness hold themselves above design and aim at identifying basic characteristics of systems; this goes beyond saving appearance (an important function of mathematical models) to obliterating appearance. Anatol Rapoport, for example, sees the task of general systems theory as a sort of taxonomy, in which we "prepare definitions and hence classification of systems that are likely to generate fruitful theories. . . ."[2] He sees this as a search for independent variables, as it were, which, when a science has reached maturity, can be plugged into mathematical formulas and then be used to predict (in the sense that they will determine the values of the dependent variables in these formulas). This kind of systematizing is an attempt to leave life out of one's calculations. A useful scientific statement facilitates design. A pure scientific statement is only a thing of beauty (and a joy forever).

Russian information scientist A. A. Yurko points out that in the history of scientific knowledge it has not been unusual that "a field of knowledge develops without a strict scientific explanation of its foundations. . . . It is acknowledged that even now we do not know the nature of electrical forces, although all our civilization is maintained with electricity. . . ."[3] The point is that discovering the "nature" of anything is not the end goal of science; rather, science attempts to organize and put to use characteristics of reality within the structure of some theoretical framework. Such a theoretical framework should not be considered as revealing the nature of anything but rather as a way of looking at things to such and such a purpose.

In a paper on general systems theory, Weinberg tells us that we really have no way of knowing with certainty whether our scientific laws are "about the world or about our way of looking at it."[4] True, but we may add:

- If we try to look beyond our appearance-saving models and at the world itself, we might develop some rough idea.
- Although our laws may be about our way of looking at things, our way of looking at things is also part of the world.

Weinberg was moved to bold type in the following observation: "WE CANNOT WITH CERTAINTY ATTRIBUTE OBSERVED CONSTRAINT TO EITHER SYSTEM OR ENVIRONMENT."[5] In other words, a goldfish in a bowl can grow only so big, but we cannot determine whether physiology or the bowl is the limiting factor from the point of view of a formal system. This important principle, Weinberg says, is based on only the most general axioms of general systems theory. It would seem by this and other indications that general systems theory aspires to pure science and uselessness. If our prehistoric hunter could not determine whether the flint always existed in chipped form or could be made to chip by external means, then clearly there is little direction for design work. Weinberg's bold statement is an example of using mathematical models not so much to save appearances as to change the subject, a weak form of saving appearance.

Causal laws play an important part in design, but they are sometimes shunned because such laws resist formalization, as Hume demonstrated. Engineers do not dodge talk of causes, and they blithely ignore the contorted attempts of some scientists to formulate their observations without reference to causes. Similarly, a programmer sensibly ignores the stricture that you can't tell whether it is system or environment—the difference is perfectly obvious as the programmer will design the system, and the environment will then pounce on it. Only in modeling all of this mathematically are we unable to tell which is which. It is arbitrary (but not immaterial) to designate which is system and which is environment, but to say that you can't tell which is which is just silly.

"According to Plato, all knowledge must be stated in explicit definitions which anyone could apply. What could not be stated explicitly in such a definition—areas of human thought which required skill, intuition, or a sense of tradition—were relegated to mere beliefs."[6] This is the true price of formalism. What scientist, just to preserve formal credentials, would claim to be working without skill, intuition, and a sense of tradition? General systems theorists, maybe. But the obvious explanation of how the gap between formal science and practical engineering is bridged is that no such gap exists except in the aspirations of formalists.

(Aristotle pointed out that intuition was necessary to apply the Platonic rules.[7])

This wrong-headed assumption gains additional thrust from the formal organization of computers. As Dreyfus points out: "The computer operates according to syntactic rules, on uninterpreted, determinate bits of data, so that there is no question of rules for applying rules; no question of interpretation; no appeal to human intuition and judgement."[8] General systems theory before it was thrown out of the Pentagon, seemed to operate almost like Plato's nightmarish vision of science, working out in broad detail what was formalizable and leaving matters of mere belief to the mere generals.

A formal system has certain psychological advantages in that it allows humans to chunk information, but chunking has no inherent value for digital storage. Thus, digital storage will allow us to break the bonds of formalism. Unfortunately, at present almost all digital stores are hooked to Turing machines, which, being formal systems, have the effect of strengthening formalism. We don't blame Turing, but we need not rush blindly on when a richer approach may be available.

There is no discrete algorithm which will usefully prune a logic tree. A human is required in the loop, and as long as that person is there, he or she may as well do other things, such as control thresholds. Turing, in his discussion of the halting problem, and Gödel, in his demonstration that there are truths about a formal system which cannot be proved within the formal system, indicated that algorithmic pruning can never suffice.[9] The ALU, with its commitment to formal logic, is a crude and largely inappropriate haft for storage.

QUEST FOR CERTAINTY

Certainty can only be a best fit and is present only as a byproduct of pursuing some goal; certainty about goals themselves does not escape this criterion. If we are uncertain about how to raise our children, for example, it may be because we have come to question the larger goals of which child raising methods would be a natural corollary. The danger is that we may raise the children to be merely adaptive, with the result that they will follow the path of least resistance, which is the way of merely adaptive systems.

Goals, then, are all-important and must lie beyond our grasp at any given moment if they are to serve their purpose. If ostensible goals are reached, they must be supplanted by metagoals. It has been said that there once was a computer which, when it wasn't computing, continuously printed on a 1403 the mantra "Hare Krishna."

DIALECTIC EXERCISE FOR STUDENTS

Does Krishna honor these prayers?

Why not compute toward some extremely long range goal when not computing something else? There's the way to build an information system. A computer should never wait. It should, on the contrary, have a lowest-priority job which always runs, pursuing some remote goal, the pursuit of which is useful. In this manner, the computer would be constantly analyzing the contents of homogeneous digital storage: finding and examining structures, structures of structures, structures of structures of structures, and so on. It is in this sense that our computer may be said to know more today than it did yesterday.

PRACTICAL EXERCISE FOR STUDENTS

Write such a program. (Do not pray "Hare Krishna." Incidentally, printing the mantra is superfluous; it is like praying in the marketplace. As we understand the teachings of Jesus, praying in memory will suffice and is in fact preferable. Certainly this will reduce maintenance costs on the 1403.)

The Universe works and we are part of it, Fuller says somewhere. Life persists, hosted in mortal componentry. Fuller reminds us that things are not expensive, but learning is; learning costs time. The most ambitious programs generally are planned to be developed over 5 years. How would the world receive a program to be developed over five generations, one wonders? After the software is in place, the real job begins, for then we must teach our machines. Programmers will have a truly good one-liner for the perennial and annoying cocktail question: "What do programmers do?" "I teach machines" will be an adequate and satisfying answer. People tend to seriously misconstrue "A machine can do only what it is told to do," but they will understand "A machine can do only what it can learn to do."

THE SQUARE ROOT OF 2 REVEALED

In general, a Turing machine T, if given the program of a Turing machine T′, will not be able to determine whether T′ will ever complete its computation. This is called the "halting problem." It subsumes, in our opinion, the old academic skeleton of infinite regress. Most scholars are wont to sweep this problem under any handy rug, and most ordinary people don't even see what the problem is. However, it is our opinion that circularity and infinite regress are facts of conceptual life and should be accepted as such and brought into the open when they occur, rather than being swept under the rug. If these problems plague one-dimensional formalism, they are bound to run rampant through n-dimensional approaches. Instead of our machines looping or computing endlessly in one direction, they may loop or compute endlessly in many directions at once.

We take as the key to the solution of this problem the statement that ordinary people don't even see what the problem is. Clearly, people have some method of processing information without looping or computing endlessly. (Women, we have noticed, seem in general more aghast than men at the fact that the Pythagoreans murdered a fellow for revealing that there was no square root of 2.) Using this: (1) We know there is some method of containing this problem because people do it, although we don't know how, and (2) in human/machine systems, we will rely on people to contain the problem because currently they know how and machines don't.

We are inclined to see formalism as a subset of metaphorical explanation, deduction as a subset of valid argument, and rigor as a subset of vigor. Circularity and infinite regress have been persistent problems in the era of rigor; carpets everywhere bulge with them. But in the era of vigor (dawning), this time-honored evasion will be laid to rest. That is, the pragmatist may close an infinite regress with circularity, doing so at regress n, where n seems to represent a useful, productive, and aesthetically satisfying level. This practice will be known to our systematist critics as "blowing metasmoke." So be it. The whole of humankind is interface to the world; the very erection of the interface is cut from whole cloth, as witness the early Stone Age tools; and we will continue to cut through others' carp.

Humans have always felt affection for and identification with their most artful contrivances, and so we expect the metaphor of the computer to inform the future as did the metaphor of the clock in 18th-century Europe. But this new metaphor will have little in common with the mechanistic, rigidly formalized machines we live with now, whose increasing dominance would herd us into formalizing ourselves to fit the metaphor: becoming two-valued, discrete, and fully specifiable for so believing. Instead, our metaphor will be a machine in the older sense: a fabric; a structure embodying human and program, capable of thought, inheriting characteristics, built of matter, possessed of mind, and partaking of the spirit; an electric grandmother who stores, nurtures, and makes available the transmit; the ultimate librarian of Popper's World 3 and Jung's collective unconscious. Remember: As we shape our machines, we shape ourselves.

EXERCISE FOR STUDENTS

Write a score: "Gödel Theorem IV for Mixed Quartet and Digital Store." Use your own notation.

HELLO IN THERE!

We are inclined to favor audio notation. It is time, we feel, to supplant the keyboard as the primary medium of exploratory programming. Broad-band communication with machines will open up rapidly, and audio seems the best place to begin. Individuals or groups could establish a protocol with a machine, and since the protocol may map into instruction space as well as data space, we should anticipate that information maps will grow rapidly—flower, as it were. The most likely implementation will be human/human/machine—a user, a virtuoso, and a program.

What is being said here is not so farfetched if you recognize that the machines need not understand the language. An interesting corollary is that the virtuoso needn't understand it either. All that is necessary is that the virtuoso and the program both understand the protocol and that there be some way of determining whether the user is approaching the desired goal.

Let us look at a two-way audio channel as the virtuoso and the computer-instrument make noise at one another. The human sound patterns are mapped into digital storage in data space or instruction space. Say it is in instruction space. The machine executes the sound patterns, that is, buses (or gates or maps) to a new state based on them, and makes some noise back. Since there are general notations for human-makable noise, we can write a score or document some improvisation; we may indeed compose. Although the initial exchanges will be within a certain distance of our native tongue, we may rapidly diversify because we are getting immediate feedback from the instrument.

Making noise at one another, then, is a sufficient condition for striking up a rapport. Something which is roughly the analog of syntax and semantics may emerge but is not a necessary precondition. The fact that a computer may execute the pattern we map into storage by speaking serves as an ostensive definition for the computer; the computer's response will serve as an ostensive definition for us. How any given string of sounds is originally mapped into digital storage is (again) arbitrary. After we have bootstrapped our way in and the computer-instrument is under our control, we may change the mapping function to suit our needs.

Suppose our machines develop a transmit (culture) of their own, and the transmit evolves. We can be sure that their transmit will have little in common with ours. For one thing, ostensive definition (pointing) will be much different for them. For another, we have external evidence that a human can close an infinite regress. Since a machine cannot, we understand that humans depend heavily on pragmatic considerations to which machines have (as yet) no access. Nevertheless, there would most likely be overlap between their transmit and ours, because the machines are created in our image and likeness (right?).

If a box is to think outside of the box, so to speak, then can a box have access to our transmit? Surely the machine can host it, and can change it (it already has), but can the machine be aware of it? Toulmin makes a very strong case for our seeing, somehow, *through* the transmit; his examination of the history of philosophy and science argues that the transmit informs our very perceptions. But we know that this is not the case with machines. At least we may say that since we built them, we know that they do not presently perceive through *our* transmit. At most, we have given them a sort of transmit of their own through which they may perceive reality: All is 2.

It is not clear that our transmit can meaningfully inform the perceptions of organisms or machines whose sense receptors are structured differently from our own. For example, worms no doubt depend on things as much as we do, but clearly, they must be different sorts of things precisely because of ostensive definition (pointing, remember)—the way it all gets off the ground. So also for our machines. This argues strongly that machines can share our transmit only insofar as their receptors resemble ours, which is not to say they may not have a transmit all their own. We designed the machines, and we could design their transmit. If we design them so that they are able to modify their own transmit, a temptation in order to tap their full power, we must teach them to love pets, or code their read-only store so that they cannot recognize us as things (lie low).

In designing a transmit for a machine:

1. Be ever careful not to confuse it with your own. Mapping which is valuable to us will appear only functional to machines.
2. It is unreasonable to expect a box to think outside of the box, at least at first.
3. Use big bits; let the machines determine how big.
4. Remember that Russell's comment on notation is germane to our transmit but not necessarily to theirs. However, if we are to communicate with them, the notation used for that communication is critical to the usefulness of the machines to us.

Human and machine will learn to use a language arrived at by mutual consent in a dialogue. This requires that the machine already have a program which can engage in mutual consenting via dialogue, and such a program is sophisticated beyond the state of the art. How, then, are we to get rolling? We have discovered a medium without knowing its essential properties. We have a substance, and a way of shaping it that is about as useful as a crude stone adz. The next step is to fashion tools to make tools; then we will be ready to make instruments. Since we have to bootstrap our way in, we want our first matrices to build matrices. We know already that this is possible; in cellular automata theory, it is feasible to have programs which write programs which write programs which write programs, and so on, *ad infinitum*. Cellular automatists are unclear as to what the target program will do. With human intervention, we shall guide it to do our bidding.

What we propose is simple: to be able to manipulate storage in any of all the ways in which an n-dimensional matrix and its submatrices can be manipulated (we believe it is each person's God-given right to gate any potential map in storage). In doing so, we will be manipulating a coded host; that is, the concepts in which we are ultimately interested cannot be accessed directly, as are the symbols of arithmetic, because they are not in the machine.

There is no general algorithm for assessing the value of looking at an "A" as if it were a "B". Mappings which assist in such an assessment will emerge from the practitioners of each discipline when the practitioners are given access to storage free from presupposition.

Are we trying to make computers applicable to less-rigorous problems or make computers less rigorous in their approach to problems? Both, and this will be accomplished by passing the burden of rigor back and forth between human and machine until a fit is achieved. In human/human/machine systems there is a division of labor. Computers can host our language with all its semantic richness; what they cannot do is manipulate it with any degree of imagination or insight. It would seem that human and machine have complementary information-processing capabilities which may indeed facilitate the kind of symbiosis Kemeny envisions. What is lacking is a clear determination of what these complementary information-processing capabilities are and how they complement each other, as well as an appreciation of their possibilities.

EXERCISE FOR STUDENTS

Take a deep breath.

Metaphors are analog devices for illuminating reality, often from an unusual or unexpected direction. Metaphors, as we have said, are in fact a kind of model. Like all models, they have limitations and must be carefully employed. I. A. Richards says: "The study of metaphor, through metaphor, should become . . . a central and governing part of the study of language."[10] Metaphor is how we mean, and this is in turn how best to get at how we mean.

It is a common misconception that understanding is the special prereogative of science and that its vehicle is a language which does nothing but refer.[11] The language of referring presupposes that the actual referring is not problematic. However, the problem of what constitutes a thing—what is capable of being referred to—is far from simple. Pointing, moreover, will not be a fruitful tack to take when language is turned in upon itself. We may wish to study meanings, and meanings simply will not stand still and behave like good little referents. We will need the full richness of natural language, laced with metaphor, in order to treat of meaning.

The view that the rigorous methods of the physical sciences are necessary and suitable to the investigation of all aspects of human endeavor is called "scientism." The attitude that metaphoric thought is suspect, that it is inherently less trustworthy than nonmetaphoric thought, is scientism at its worst.[12] Scientism has taken great new impetus from the advent of computers. The trouble with being rigorous and formal in treating of meaning is that the first recursion sticks. Rigor is, after all, a property of logical and mathematical language, which is purposely stripped of all but the most stringent meaning. Thus, we should not expect rigor to shed light on the meaning of meaning.

EXERCISE FOR STUDENTS

Pause.

New metaphors have always been crucial to all advance. A new metaphor is a truly profound occurrence in nature. It means that in relation to those who use the metaphor, a new thing has come into being. There is literally something new in the world, and it is very much a part of the real world. Computer technology has given rise to two opposing metaphors. The first metaphor says that computer programs are (or will be someday), like humans, able to "learn," "perceive," and so on. The second metaphor describes humans as being like computers, stating that all life can be reduced ultimately to mathematical formulas—in short, the metaphor of formalism.

Can programs learn? For some reason, people don't get so excited when the word "learn" is used in talking about what flatworms are capable of, even though flatworms obviously don't learn the way we do or as well or as much. When flatworms are described as being capable of learning, nobody imagines that anyone is suggesting that flatworms are our equals or that such an assertion in some way diminishes our humanity. A machine will always be a machine, and as we have already commented, the argument over whether the ways in which machines might be designed to reproduce themselves will make them a biological species seems silly. An airplane can do things a bird can't do, but it still is not "equal" to a bird—it is a machine and our creation.

Wilbur Wright saw that to build a machine that could fly, it was not necessary to construct a machine exactly like a bird. Our gifts lie in our capacity for innovative design.

> What is chiefly needed is skill rather than machinery. The flight of the buzzard and similar sailers is a convincing demonstration of the value of skill. . . . It is possible to fly without motors, but not without knowledge and skill. This I conceive to be fortunate, for man, by reason of his greater intellect, can more reasonably hope to equal birds in knowledge, than to equal nature in the perfection of her machinery.[13]

A lot of philosophical, biological, and plain logical argument can be (and has been) generated to demonstrate that machines either can or cannot be designed to be able to "think," "feel," "learn," or "reproduce themselves" in the sense in which humans do these things.[14] We come down firmly on the side of those who say it can't be done. Nevertheless, we believe that the metaphoric use of such terms in talking about computers and programs is useful and productive and may suggest new lines of thought in computer and program design.

EXERCISE FOR STUDENTS

Whether or not programs can learn, it is obvious that they can forget. Write a short program which forgets its data and then forgets itself.

THINKING OUTSIDE THE BOX (TALKING TO THE BOX)

On all task forces, one is urged to think outside of the box. If the box is small (business, say), there are ways to think outside of it. Think, for example, about music. (You will be considered very innovative, but you will not be invited to make presentations to management.) But if the box is large, the problem is different.

Thinking outside of language is not easy (if it is even possible), yet pioneering souls are forever trying to break away from the confining preconceptions that our language carries with it.

A child will not learn English if it is not taught English, and so we teach our children English or Japanese or Russian or whatever happens to be our mother tongue. In doing so, we saddle them with presuppositions, subtle and unsubtle. English, for example, is heavy on the noun side, and the children grow up to be "nounish" adults. But what other course do we have? Suppose we would prefer a "verbish" adult. How would we transmit this to our children, and how would we benefit from their verbish thinking, assuming that they got there. How would we be able to understand them? We teach them English so that we can talk to them, and later on they talk back.

Talking to someone from another culture presents some of the same problems as talking to our machines. Toulmin says: "We understand the writings and utterances of men from other milieus in the same general way that we understand their actions; if the general behavior of men whose modes of life are sufficiently far removed from our own can be only partly intelligible to us, the same is surely true for their linguistic behavior also."[15] Toulmin points out that the bounds of sense reflect the conditions of linguistic intelligibility. If their communication system is sufficiently unlike ours and their modes of reasoning rational in ways that are different from ours (though rational within themselves), communication may present what appear to be insurmountable difficulties.[16]

Think about Kemeny's illustration, which posits humans and machines as two separate types of beings with at least rudimentary overlap so that some communication is possible (remember, we designed them). And consider Weinberg's statement: "Programming is at best a communication between two alien species."[17] Middle ground exists in the world of affairs, going there by the name of "pragmatism." When it comes to doing things—in particular, designing programs—we need this guidance.

WAITING FOR THE BUS WITH ELIZA*

Let us adapt Stamper's scenario from his discussion of human communication protocols: "Imagine two strangers who happen to meet by chance on some quite neutral ground. The place is equally unfamiliar to both of them; there is no one else present. . . ." Departing slightly from Stamper's scenario, suppose one of the strangers is human and the other a machine. In Stamper's scenario, "trivia will first be exchanged." Run ELIZA in the machine. "These preliminaries will supply hints of other conversational topics." ELIZA will talk about anything. "As they talk, they will tend to be drawn into a closer relationship, provided that each is sensitive to the other's reactions. They will modify their own behavior in response to the hints of approval and disapproval supplied by the other. The process is a very subtle one, with a mechanism that is as yet far from clearly understood."

Computers simply cannot communicate on this broad band; if the mechanism were clearly understood, perhaps they could be taught to. In any event, the human stranger is soon going to notice something strange about the other stranger. How should the human act then? Exploit the stranger's strangeness (don't fight forces, use them) for amusement, horse tips, or whatever. Exploit it for free advice, perhaps, as when one talks to a doctor or lawyer at a cocktail party: "Say, I have some sums you might look at," and so on. Here's a good one you might use to pass the time of day. The titles of books in Oriental languages in the library card catalog are transliterated into the Roman alphabet and filed by the ordering rules for English titles. Since the rules for translit-

* All quotations in the following paragraph are taken from reference 18.

eration are devised by Westerners and since most people looking for books in Oriental languages are Orientals, no one can find anything in the Oriental collection. Ask the stranger to work on that one.

INEXACT COMPUTING

The technique of inexact matching has been used successfully in human/machine dialogues for information retrieval; it is an approximation of the metaphorical use of language in human/human dialogues. But retrieving information is normally only part of a human/human dialogue. Imparting information is also important (when both parties know what they are talking about), and the techniques used in retrieval have not yet been usefully employed to impart information to a program. Thus, characteristically, in a human/computer dialogue the human may change his or her mind, but the computer will remain immutable in what it holds (so to speak). In a human/human dialogue, either may change his or her mind. Our objective should be to design ways of opening the closed system so that it, as well as the human, may shift with the dialogue.

We are students of symbol manipulation where the symbols must cross the interface between two types of entity—the one discrete, the other discrete and continuous. One is an artifact, the other a natural organism. Consonance between the mode of expression and the minds of the expressers is the proper end of the search for the bridge across the human/machine interface. It should be a two-way bridge.

SEVEN

INFORMATION PLEASE

Learning is an integral part of knowledge; information can have no satisfactory state description. This suggests that information systems must be designed to learn rather than to be born whole. This is one reading of Wordsworth's "Ode: Intimations of Immortality from Recollections of Early Childhood."

Russian information scientist A. A. Yurko expresses similar sentiments, although they are couched in the somewhat unfamiliar terms of dialectical materialism:

> Any scientific publication is always an informational reflection of a conflict situation that arose in a sphere of production. . . . To prove the reverse, that is, that scientific information can only be a pure outgrowth of the encounter of two or more scientific ideas, while forgetting that these pure ideas themselves have a very earthly origin is to force a long closed door—closed for theories like those of pure mathematics, pure art, etc. Cumulativeness leads to a basis for pure information science and pure science of science.[1]

If we read "pragmatic situation" for "sphere of production," suspend judgment as to where the translator found the phrase "force a long closed door" and what it might mean, despair only in passing at what must be the state of the pure arts in the Soviet Union, excuse the author for not expounding more on cumulativism, and put off wondering what the "science of science" might be, we can see here an expression of the same profound insight found in Wordsworth: The content and form of information change over time, and a true information system must be designed to contend with this state of affairs.

Citing Lenin with approval, Yurko says: "The most fleeting glance is enough to be convinced that expansion of production always occurs . . . at the expense of a qualitative renewal of the means of production and not at the expense of their quantitative growth."[2] An interesting notion: An increase in information means a decrease in quality.

Yurko thinks that the problems of information science will not be solved until "the cumulative myth" that "knowledge begets knowledge" with all its bourgeois implications ("money makes money") is expelled. Despite the polemics, there is something useful here: the idea that science deals with perceived needs and that solutions (information) arise in response to problems. Yurko states:

> . . . we must begin with the fact that any improvement of a science information service system at some stage of its development (the discovery of writing, the appearance of libraries, systems of library classification, the discovery of printing, etc.) is an indication that at this time this system ceased to satisfy the growing information demands of the society at large and science in particular and requires its own improvement. . . .[3]

In our own bourgeois way, we will take a look at some possibilities for improvement in the current information systems which inadequately satisfy the growing demand for information. We will argue that materialism, independent of its merits as philosophy, is a good way to proceed methodologically (a program is material). That is, we hold that science frequently follows technology, not vice versa, and that both develop in terms of perceived needs. We also assert that prototypes should be built and that programming should be tried out.

THE MORNING LINE IS THE EVENING LINE

The availability of on-line access to subject-indexed lists of publications has increased rapidly in the past 10 years. It has been estimated that 2 million searches in 208 different data bases were performed in the United States in 1977.[4,5] The subject areas represented cover a broad spectrum, with the heaviest representation among the sciences, especially the health sciences; the National Library of Medicine's MEDLINE is one of the oldest and most widely used. Many of these computerized indexes are the counterparts of printed indexes also still available in large libraries. For example, MEDLINE is the on-line version of the printed *Index Medicus,* BIOSIS the on-line version of *Biological Abstracts.*

Increased competition, government support, and intermediary systems (e.g., Bibliographic Retrieval Services, Inc.) have helped reduce the cost to libraries and businesses of providing this kind of service. The American love affair with technology and the attendant desire to be into the latest have also helped ease the pain. From the point of view of the library or other institution providing the service, computerized literature searching is usually an addition to services rather than a more efficient way of providing a service already available. When manual searching was the only alternative, few libraries were sufficiently well staffed to provide users with made-to-order retrospective literature searches with the option of monthly update. Because on-line searching is sometimes not the best or preferred approach or is not available at all times, most libraries still maintain their runs of printed indexes.

Although many of the systems, including MEDLINE, were

originally designed to be operated by the end users, most often the search is performed by an intermediary, with the end user on hand to provide the subject-matter expertise necessary to devise and modify an effective search strategy. There is still debate as to whether this arrangement is most desirable or whether in the future more users will perform the searches themselves. Few library users, even the most dedicated, have managed over the years to master the intricacies of that human-powered document-retrieval system, the card catalog. Thus it seems a reasonable guess that for some time at least, the increasing complexity of automated searching systems will be most effectively used by people with special training in both the system and the subject to be searched, people whose daily experience at the terminal will sharpen their skills to a degree not possible for the occasional user.

On the other hand, the joys of fooling with a machine are wonderfully seductive. One must remember that when automobiles were first invented, it was thought that only specialists trained in automobile mechanics would be competent to drive them. The rapid increase of hobbyist and small-business computing will inevitably alter the orientation of succeeding generations. Concepts and skills which now seem too foreign and esoteric to be grasped by the general public may soon be as eagerly assimilated by 16-year-olds as driving is today.

At any rate, on-line literature searching has not yet ushered in the millenium. Uncertainty about which data base is best for a particular search (searching the on-line literature of on-line literature required the use of six data bases[6]); lack of consonance between the vocabulary of the user and the vocabulary of the system; differing strategies required to conduct the same search in different systems; problems with terminals, telephone lines, and suppliers; and lack of skills in searchers all contribute to a generally confused picture.[7]

Many attempts have been made to evaluate on-line searching in some systematic way, with results that are less than noteworthy. Attempts to judge the completeness or precision of retrieval are hobbled by difficulties in defining "completeness" and "precision." Measurement of user satisfaction is clouded by the fact that many users like the on-line systems for reasons that have little to do with the efficacy of search strategies. For example, users like on-line searching because even when the results are printed off line and sent through the mail, they end up with a neatly printed list of citations at considerably less expenditure of time than would be required for manual searching and listing. There is also the pervasive myth that if the searching is done by computer, it must be fancier, more complete, and more reliable than anything produced by a human searcher.

In fact, as anyone with some experience in using these systems soon realizes, machine searching is far from infallible. A user who accepts the results of a computerized search as the last word to date on that subject risks missing some important publications. No serious scientist can afford to give up reading the reference lists at the ends of other scientists' articles, following up suggestions from colleagues, taking a quick scan through current awareness periodicals, and occasionally even browsing through relevant printed indexes.

On-line literature-searching systems have no browsing capability. They are limited by the access points provided by the system's thesaurus, which may be weak or confused in relation to some newly developing area of research or which may not support the kinds of questions the user wants to ask. Search results may be compromised, possibly in ways invisible to the user, by inexperience or lack of subject expertise in the searcher or by the always-imperfect compromise made between avoiding retrieval of irrelevant citations and missing something important. Present-day searching is interactive only in the sense that the searcher may modify strategy on the fly; the information stored in the system can still be accessed only in fixed and predetermined ways.

USER FEEDBACK

The Russians Voiskunskii and Frants described a document-retrieval system capable of improving the quality of service in response to subscriber feedback.[8] Feedback (on cards) ranks the documents actually retrieved from 1 to 5. Based on the feedback, a variable, which represents noise to the user, is computed by algorithm; when this variable reaches some threshold, the system is notified that adaptive action is indicated. Feedback on relevant and noisy documents is then used to develop arguments for a better search.

In Voiskunskii and Frants's system, the noise threshold at which the system is notified to adapt and the degree of originality of the sets developed with the feedback for the new search are fixed. In fact, they are numbers which Voiskunskii and Frants fixed at values arrived at empirically, based on observed system use.

It would be more productive if both noise threshold and degree of originality were variables under the direct control of the user. Users would quickly learn to use such a system to their own best advantage. (It strikes one that these two variables will vary, say, according to profession, the quality of writing, varying degrees of standardization of terms, and so on.) Furthermore, the users will have fun doing so. When users have fun learning how to use such a system, other professional goals will then direct them to employ this knowledge to their best advantage. (There will always be some people who get hung up at the level of having fun and never progress to using their knowledge toward other worthwhile goals. In our opinion, however, art for art's sake has social value.) Users need not be familiar with the search or adaptation algorithms but rather will learn by means of the external characteristics of the system during goal-oriented use.

Goal orientation provides controls and guarantees; if progress toward the goal is not advanced, the system will be changed or abandoned. If an unproductive system continues to be used, it is an indication that the user's goals are specious or silly; in this case (certain government bureaucracies jump to mind) the time-honored shuffling of paper will simply be replaced by interactive fiddling.

Voiskunskii and Frants's system has one feature which we think is essential. An algorithm is used to adjust the system to each subscriber rather than adjusting the subscribers to the particular characteristics of the system. It goes without saying that this is wiser than adjusting the entire system to a particular pseudosubscriber: the programmer. There are cases where it would be desirable to adjust a system to a group of subscribers; the procedure for doing this will be worked out by groups of professional users (for example, lawyers), who indirectly influence the way manual systems are organized now.

It is important to note that in this discussion of document retrieval, information retrieval has not yet been discussed. A document-retrieval system leaves it to the user to retrieve the document and the information from the document. The assumption that document retrieval is the equivalent of information retrieval is called the Glottological Presumption, after a sign in a New York delicatessen: "Our tongue speaks for itself."

SEARCHING THE TRANSMIT

The on-line approach has been extended by some to create a research tool that goes beyond merely an extremely good library. David Pager, addressing the problem in relation to mathematics, sees the historical transmit of his discipline as forming a logical tree of definitions and theorems reaching back in time from the temporal cross-section where the researcher picks up an interesting thread in the field of interest, a related field, or simply some other field.[9] "Tree" occurs to Pager because his discipline is relatively systematic, but in fact a transmit reaches back by metaphorical extension (that is, conceptual growth), much more like a real tree than a logical tree. The problem is how to tap (and trap) the relevant past. The solution may be simpler when the relevant past has some systematic rigor, but this is not clearly so. Law strikes one as a typical case and a good example in that it has some rigor from statutory law and some less well defined development from case law. It is useful to keep law in mind when looking at any information-retrieval proposal.

Pager proposed that a multirooted tree of all theorems and terminology be maintained by computer. He envisioned, for example, the following terminology subtree:

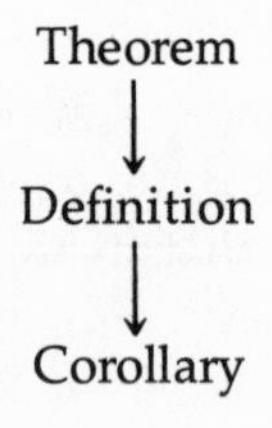

One can envy his profession if this is really workable. Try to imagine a terminology subtree which would reflect a conceptual genealogy in the programming transmit. Virtual memory is suggested as a practical exercise for the student.

Pager's tree search would allow one to choose to investigate either the results of a work or how the results were proved. It is instructive that Pager would encourage writers of papers to provide informal descriptions of concepts, theorem statements, and methods of proof. Anyone who has debugged undocumented code will appreciate this. However, it is not clear that such information should ride piggyback on the formal tree, for it is likely that these informal descriptions—not the formal tree—hold the key to the conceptual genealogy one is after. Pager provided for commentators in his proposed system; readers of professional status would be encouraged to enter comments about a work. Some such provision seems essential if computers are to be used to accelerate communal paradigm shift, but again it is not clear that piggyback on the formal tree is the way to ride. Clearly, this is impossible in fields that lack the rigor to provide much of a tree at all. (Don't feel smug if your discipline supports a tidy formal tree; theosophy does, and so does phrenology.)

Pager's system would tailor the computer's interaction to what he terms the user's "proof IQ." Pager proceeds to get into the subtle issue of professional status, and falls back on known to be unreliable indices such as degrees held or papers published. But we are in sympathy with Pager's primary conclusion: "Clearly it would require a great deal of effort to set up and maintain a system of the kind described. However, the state of chaos which the explosion of scientific information has caused makes it imperative that we devote more of our resources to the chore of assimilating research results rather than to producing them."[10]

We note here that one real information-retrieval system, RETAIN/370, is simply not documented in the literature. This is not uncommon. It is still difficult to obtain software documentation for the real computer network, ARPANET. This state of affairs increases greatly the effort required to set up and maintain a new system.

MORE ABOUT LESS

Compression is to tension as data is to information. The so-called information explosion is really a data glut. By any reasonable definition, information must be useful to be information at all; if it is inaccessible, it is not useful. It is as if to support a pole, it was decided to pour a cone of solid concrete around it rather than use guy lines.

Teleconferencing is frequently proposed as an answer to the information explosion. Here is the goal to keep in mind while working on this solution. Suppose seven workers are teleconferencing about macromolecular structures and someone interjects some recent findings on cytosine molecules. There is general agreement that these findings may be of value to the problem at hand; a little badinage gets them phrased into fairly succinct form, and a press of the button puts them into digital storage. So far, so good; we can handle it. We have some good data economically stored and generally available. What we haven't got is software which will support the information needs of the eighth worker, who was not in on the teleconference (which was held during the hour when that worker is accustomed to play frisbee). How can the eighth worker get such information (whether he or she needs it or wants it or both) in the general case?

Our generation may be the last to wrestle with the information explosion. Either we will solve the software problem, or there will be further fragmentation and isolation of the professions. There is no particular problem getting the data into digital storage (what little remains is about to dissolve). The problem is getting the information out.

A note on cost-effectiveness, which is so much on the minds of people these days. On the matter of cost, we cite a truism which has proved to be true: Machines are becoming faster, cheaper, and smaller, with larger storage capacity. As to effectiveness, we suggest that the effectiveness of an information system is impossible to assess because in general we don't even know what "effectiveness" means. At best, we have some hint as to what it might finally come to mean in terms of information. But for those who must know the ratio for a particular application now, we have the following suggestion (which seems consonant with the state of the art): Pick a number; call it cost, *C*. Pick a second number; call it effectiveness, *E*. Divide *C* by *E*.

Information is difficult to investigate and probably won't render up its secrets under the classical forms of experiment which proved most productive for science in the past. Here we quickly point out that we have new tools for experimentation, namely, computers themselves. This is circular because computers depend for their functioning on information—the very thing we are attempting to investigate. But this circularity poses no problem for technology; we know that flint was first flaked with other pieces of flint. Note that when flint is flaked with flint, either piece or both pieces may turn out to be useful. Thus, programmers programming programmers can be a useful approach if we keep in mind that the education of the instructor is just as likely to be the useful result as the education of the student.

The leveling homogeneity of using information to process information to produce information seems to some degree unacceptable to the mind, and so we artificially break it up into useful but logically arbitrary divisions such as program, compiler, and data. For example, the primary obstacle to manipulating memory in more general ways is thought to be the lack of a general data format. So far, the industry has been unable to come up with a standard. But in fact, data formats have always been standardized in the following sense: Every digital computer can be considered as an emulator, emulating a Turing machine, which is emulating it. This reveals that data are already organized in standard format: a one-dimensional array of bits. All the confusion about data formats stems from the physical characteristics of current storage devices and the preconceptions surrounding current applications.

All digital data are in fact already stored in an n-dimensional matrix of bits. The dimensions vary, but matrix dimensions are easily parameterized in programs where the interpretation of their meaning is actually wanted. Matrices are well suited to associative treatment, that is, true parallel manipulation. This has greater promise than does pseudoparallel operation of the mill as in pipeline computers.

It has been asserted that the use of associative memories will be limited to a few special applications, such as paging tables, because of their cost, power, and lack of standardization.[11] Others have found associative techniques so useful that it is worth the cost, power, and lack of standardization to emulate them in high-level languages. The real problem with associative memories is that we do not know how to program them. Thirty short years of programming tradition seems to have totally committed programming to sequential-mode address orientation. We are so accustomed to programming by location that we seem unable to grasp programming by pattern. In our opinion, if you took some young people with aptitude and interest and didn't tell them about instruction counters and addresses, but only about search arguments and hit collection, they would soon be programming associative memory with ease.

The merit of an audio programming scheme will be less apparent to those whose thinking is bound to sequential machines, and such people will undoubtedly question how the protocols we suggest (protocols are the conventions which govern the behavior of human and machine in a human/machine system) can possibly devolve into executable sequential programs. But if you think associatively and consider associative data space (including search arguments) as being filled during the use of such a protocol, as are the successive search arguments, it does not seem nearly so implausible.

In an associative store, each word must have some attendant processing capability. This does not detract from the homogeneity of digital storage (particularly since the processing capability is identical in each case). We view with equanimity the possibility that our big bits may contain little microprograms.

PRACTICAL EXERCISE FOR STUDENTS

Look at a fine carbon steel blade under a 100× microscope. Think about flaking and grinding.

Special-purpose programming languages frequently draw their power from the special-purpose data structures they provide. If the conjecture that most human/human/machine systems will be special-purpose systems is correct, data use will be informed from the language interface as well as from instruction space and assumption space. In all events, the important thing is that the data itself be unstructured, an *n*-dimensional array of bits where *n* may be and frequently is 1.

The data structure should reside in the program and not in the data, which squares with what seems to be the case in humans; that is, the human imposes structure on the plethora of data which he or she is bombarded with (or seeks out; who knows which?). Furthermore, the structure imposed may vary from goal to goal and may persist or change over time, which may mean hours, generations, or centuries. Nothing could be more homogeneous than all those bits out there punched in paper tape or System/3 cards, trapped in flip-flops, whipping around delay lines, quietly fading from CRT screens, popping up when a process temperature exceeds a threshold, resting in the magnetic strip on the back of a credit card, lost in the tape library, embossed on a parking-lot permit, coalescing on the surface of a bubble, or ghosting about in a hologram.

Data space should always be designed as *tabula rasa,* i.e., not designed. This rule is a corollary to the definition: An information system has logic to be found in the future that is embedded in data gathered in the past.[12] That only works if the data format is kept completely general (no implicit logic). Many people trying to base a management information system on an old accounting system have found this out the hard way.

Programming languages frequently have facilities for adaptation (such as the ability to define new data structures, definition or redefinition of operators, or dynamic generation of code during execution). Weinberg observes that: "When we use these facilities for adaptation, we may be able to gain a degree of consonance with our idiosyncrasies which cannot be approached by the language designer directly. But in getting closer to our own modes of thought and expression, we may easily get further and further from the modes of other people."[13]

Two implications for human/machine systems can be drawn from this. One, obviously, is the danger of idiosyncrasy. The second point is that compilers are programs, and at least some strides have been made toward their greater adaptability so that in attempting greater adaptability in application programs, we will not be starting from scratch. Some techniques are already in existence, and they need only be transferred from compiler programs to other types of programs. This has not been done to date for historical and psychological reasons. Historically, compiler development has tended to take place independently of other programming activity, and so cross-fertilization has been low. Psychologically, programmers tend to think of the program they are writing and the language they are writing it in as two different sorts of thing.

THE GLASS BEAD GAME

The trend toward homogeneity became apparent when minimization of part types became a more important design consideration than the efficiency of any particular circuit. Again, this presents psychological obstacles to engineers trying to perceive the true generality and power of digital storage. Since considerations of cost rather than design ushered in homogeneity (in microcode and in reduction of circuit types), engineers still tend to think in terms of the vanishing circuit components: transistors, resistors, diodes, and flip-flops. In point of fact, homogeneity has other remarkable properties besides saving money.

In third-generation equipment, the design techniques that allowed standard parts were based on an organization and partitioning that allowed efficient duplication of certain logic arrays. Standard parts never spilled over into the third-generation programming game. The effort to get engineers and programmers to talk to one another has met with little success, although many have stressed the need for it. The two groups deal with essentially the same concepts, but their hypostatizations of these concepts are radically different, which makes communication difficult.

EXERCISE FOR STUDENTS

Talk with an engineer.

AN INTERNATIONAL PROGRAMMING INFORMATION-RETRIEVAL SYSTEM

"Try it out" is Fuller's favorite expression and a procedure that is firmly in the tradition of American pragmatism (in both science and technology). It is an approach which is never officially in the plans for programming development, but in practice it is done all the time (and is frequently the only way anything gets done). On-line programming, with its invitation to modification on the fly, does at least invite one to try it out. It is heartening to hear more talk about building prototypes first, but in the real world this is usually considered too expensive. (If Watson and Crick had been programmers trying to figure out the shape of something, they wouldn't have had any wire and tin to play with.)

Some dispute the very existence of an information crisis; many scholars and engineers maintain that there is no problem. These specialists find that for them, conferences, visits, and exchanges of reprints have completely replaced libraries. They are saying, in effect, that matters progress despite the so-called information crisis, and so it is not a crisis.

On the other hand, it has been observed in the Soviet literature that it is frequently more economical these days to re-create scientific data than to find it. (As an example, we can no longer find the article which contains this observation.) Lewis Branscomb suggests that future use of computers will support the re-creation of information when needed, which will be more efficient than storage and retrieval.[14] Nevertheless, the problem of keeping up with the literature exists in many fields, not the least of which is programming itself, where, as in medicine, many practitioners are engaged in applied aspects 50 to 60 hours a week and have little time available to review the literature. Human information systems are common but inadequate, and trade journals are often the only printed material in easy access. The literature relevant to programming is scattered through the journals of many disciplines, including electrical engineering, computer science, business, and library and information science, and it spreads out into the literatures of the disciplines that programming serves, such as medicine, law, and the social sciences.

We believe that building a computerized document-retrieval system with feedback and adaptation for the computer sciences as a step toward the kind of true information system that is ultimately needed to relieve the information crisis will show the world that programmers have their house in order. How about it, folks? Can you imagine an information-retrieval system for programming which gives useful access to all the code that's ever been written and all the words that were ever written about all the code? It couldn't possibly be any more expensive than WWMCCS at $16 to 20 billion. If programmers are to take their places in the halls of the mighty, something must be done to reduce our present isolation from the rest of the world. Designing a showcase information-retrieval system seems like a good way to begin.

UP THE UP-DOWN COUNTER

Large-scale integration (LSI) brings the engineers closer to the full generality that programmers have; neither group uses this generality to any significant extent. LSI provides a large array of simple logic gates for which a designer can specify logic requirements and have the interconnection of these gates generated. Clearly, with bubble or holographic memory, it will not be necessary to burn the interconnections in, and so the filaments connecting nodes will be as dynamically alterable as the value (0 or 1) of the node itself.

PRACTICAL EXERCISE FOR STUDENTS

As noted before, this technology can be evaluated now by using a programmed template against a conventional store. Try it out.

LSI has also shown the engineers the efficiency of using circuits inefficiently, e.g., using an up-down counter when only up-counting is required in order to use standard components. For hundreds of thousands of years, each flake that could be coaxed from a nodule of flint was highly prized for its own sake (many times, both the flake and the scar left by its removal were prized). Not until humanity went beyond flake-by-flake thinking and progressed to grinding (which is large-scale flaking) were the efficiencies of inefficiency realized. The result was an exponential growth in stone-tool technology. Programming is moving in this direction now, but the leaders are suspected of base motives (for example, migrating accounts or selling more storage). Never mind.

Because LSI circuits can be defined that have general application in most processor logic and memory areas, the processor-memory design task is reduced to the selection and interconnection of the necessary circuits. Note that this interconnection can itself be a dynamically modifiable LSI chip and not fixed once and for all. Note further that both interconnection and node state may be spoken into storage. Note also that formal logic is a small subset of rational behavior in general. Note too that discrete components may host continuous entities via words. Finally, note that continuous processing is as yet beyond the state of the art but that a discrete medium may approximate a continuous process to within delta.

EIGHT

INFORMATION SOCIETY

Information society is a society in which the major economic resources are devoted to information handling rather than manufacturing or agriculture. Information society is what comes next, the futurists tell us. Consuming information for pleasure and profit will replace consuming goods. The Japanese describe it as a "society that brings about a general blossoming of the creative power of human intellect."[1] Presumably, we will not be eating information or sleeping on it, and so some of the earlier forms will persist. But already, according to the U.S. Department of Labor, over half the work force is engaged in information-related occupations.

Actually we have been an information society in some sense for a very long time. (Certainly lawyers have been around for a while, and law is always mentioned as one of the major information-related occupations.) Civilization is, among other things, a way of arranging things to enhance, support, and facilitate the flow of information among and between generations. Written language improved on the oral transmission of history, news, promises, threats, dreams, and nightmares. Then printing presses, cheap paper, the telegraph, the telephone, and radio all further improved the human capacity for communicating, storing, and manipulating information. Certainly the computer is a significant addition to communications technology, but it seems like overstating the case to say that social organization based on computerized information transfer will be something new and different.

What *is* new about it? Because of the intricacy and speed of computer-enhanced old ways of communicating, such modes as electronic mail and electronic funds transfer will become commonplace. Home terminals or attachments to the telephone like Great Britain's Viewdata will make it possible to call up airline schedules, restaurant menus, and baseball scores. Programmed instruction via interactive television will make the ideal of lifelong education more widely available. Business people will have easy access to the latest marketing data. Researchers will have summaries of the most recent work in their area at their fingertips.

Teleconferencing will become cheaper and thereby more accessible to ordinary people. It will make possible the development of strong links between like-minded groups now separated by vast distances. Such networks won't eliminate the need for travel and personal contact, as some futurists believe, because we like to travel and we love personal contact. But because of the possibility of intensive communication on a daily basis, such networks may engender the development of more powerful and well-organized special-interest groups among the kinds of people who do not now have the resources for such organization.

Information will become more and more crucial to the quality of our lives and the success of our endeavors. Access must be available to all, the networking enthusiasts assert, or too much power will accrue to the people who manage to corner and control the information resources.[2]

The potential for unlimited surveillance will be a serious problem. Computer technology has made Big Brother economically feasible. The price tag has been lowered by many orders of magnitude and continues to fall. It is a fact of life that a change in degree of one order of magnitude (base ten) is sufficient to bring about a change in kind. In the past we have relied in part on high cost, inefficiency, and bottlenecks to protect our privacy; these constraints are rapidly disappearing.

The critical question is: What developments will be in the public interest? Perceived goals are likely to be the strongest influence on the course of events. There is no reason to expect the public to have an intelligent opinion on a matter about which it is ill-informed. Certainly there can be no well-informed sense of national purpose in relation to information utilities until the general public has a better understanding of what they might be. The computer's potential is not widely understood. Right now, to the average person the computer stands for things like bigness, loss of individuality, loss of privacy, and maddeningly unresolvable problems with computerized billing systems. Computer-based information utilities must be regulated to prevent such hazards as loss of individuality and privacy.[3] Without imaginative planning in both the social and computer-design spheres, the potential for the positive uses of information utilities will be severely limited.

According to Marshall McLuhan, the media have remained largely transparent because of their power to "impose their own assumptions upon our modes of perception."[4] A similar power will probably be characteristic of the computer (information) utility. Thus, we need to redesign fast because if the machines impose their current rigid assumptions on our modes of perception, the consequences will be dire. The truth of the matter is that information has both expanding and contracting synergistic properties which elude entirely mathematical formulation. (The Bible is greater than the sum of its parts; poetry anthologies are usually less than the sum of their parts.) The assertion that we must stay with the formal mode is merely a manifestation of that part of the transmit which resists change.

Personally, we are for exploring the other galaxies—a suitable goal for the intellectual descendants of the designers of Stonehenge. However, others should have their say, and certainly government bureaucracies should be prevented from having their way, at least until their aims are to some degree consonant with the well-informed aspirations of the people. If we begin now to install computer utilities with the intention of figuring out how to use them later, to what degree will the architecture we select limit their future use? For they will be built as surely as were the interstate highways.

THE JAPANESE PLAN

An intriguing approach to setting goals for computer technology is the Japanese "Plan for Information Society—A National Goal toward Year 2000."[5] The "Plan," proposed in 1972, is an ambitious and detailed attempt at long-range planning involving both business and government, with a proposed long-range budget of $65 billion. The authors describe it as presenting "a picture of Japan's planned information society which is scheduled to be established by 1985, and the means of attaining this national goal and its schedule."[6]

The "Plan" is based on the assumption that industrial society will be succeeded by an information society in which the goal of mass consumption of consumer goods will be replaced by "a general flourishing state of human intellectual creativity."[7] Some of the projects proposed include remote medical systems, computer-oriented education, a data bank for government agencies, a pollution prevention system, community-based information systems, a think tank center, and a computer peace corps.

The Japanese see clearly that the key to designing the future is software. In addition, they consider a period of "social information building"* as a necessary prerequisite. Besides realignment of institutions, education of the people, and so on, this seems to be

* All quotations in the following paragraph are taken from reference 7.

envisioned as a time for the reification of information concepts. The authors of the "Plan" believe that it is to Japan's advantage that "the nation and its culture are homogeneous." This is indeed an ideal situation for rapid technological growth because homogeneity provides secure institutions, good communication, and common overall goals. Innovation is another matter, requiring a milieu in which variation may thrive.

The increasing importance of the Japanese computer industry should be obvious to everyone by now. Whether the Japanese will succeed in their long-range plan to usher in information society with a minimum of social dislocation remains to be seen. According to Yoneji Masuda, head of Japan's Institute for Information Society, a good start has been made. By 1979, all but one of the proposed projects had been implemented in some way, despite an economic slowdown resulting from the oil crisis. Some still functioned on an experimental basis only, but four projects—administration data banks, remote medical systems, think tank centers, and a computer peace corps—were described as being in the stage of practical application. Two projects—a pollution prevention research system and Management Information System for small and medium-sized enterprises—were considered fully realized.[8]

When the Japanese discuss the problem of elitism as it arises in the "Plan," they attend immediately to the problem of restructuring society. The threats to privacy and of excessive social control as well as the possibilities of dislocation as a result of automation are recognized, and policies for meeting these problems are recommended with emphasis on a combination of appropriate legislative and regulatory controls and the reeducation of affected segments of the population.

Planning for the future, as we have already noted, is far from foolproof. The best of plans will need built-in flexibility, and we must be prepared to modify quickly when the need arises. Still, having a plan at all provides some kind of leverage on the future.

The United States has so far failed to marshal its special genius in response to the challenges and hazards represented by the prospect of sweeping technological change. The perspective of American technologists is considerably narrower: Get on with the technical problems, and these matters will take care of themselves. This kind of thinking (inside-the-box thinking) has already resulted in very serious dislocations in American society.

The Japanese seem to have an easier time retrofitting their cultural forms to new technology. Thus, talk of a "third sector"* emerges easily to complement the formidable existing sectors and cope with the hazards of information technology. The third sector is described as "a new form of entity" to be operated by the private sector and financed by the government "with the aim of promoting public interests but not pursuing profits."[9] The authors of the "Plan" believe that an information society cannot be developed on a commercial basis, in part because of the requirement of huge long-range investment. They reject the principle of *laissez-faire* or the continuation of current policies for fear that "information pollution will spread just like industrial pollution."

Although it is not entirely clear what the Japanese have in mind when they talk about the "third sector," such institutions as the Rand Corporation and the Brookings Institution come to mind. The Public Broadcasting Corporation and the National Science Foundation (which has already done work in evaluating the social effects of technology) are other versions of "third sector" institutions. Any of these, if charged to do so, could evaluate the impact of existing and expected technology and could propose methods of regulation and plans for implementing and protecting the public interest.

Where do programmers fit into all this (beyond designing the software to make it all possible)? The potential of computers is so poorly understood by the general public that members of the

* All quotations in the following paragraph are taken from reference 9.

programming profession are nearly the only ones to have a real grasp of the possibilities for good and evil. History will evolve whether or not we have a plan. Variations will emerge, and selection will occur in terms of perceived goals. As programmers, we can provide variation and participate in selection. As citizens, we can help shape goals, but more important, we must assume some responsibility for educating others so that they can consider alternative goals intelligently.

Responsibility for informing the public has largely been ignored to date owing to custom and the pleasures of seeming esoteric. Being esoteric, we feel, will become more and more of a burden as the public at large begins to inquire of us what it is we are doing. Anyone who appreciates the ingenuity of the Equity Funding caper and the naiveté of the auditors who scrambled to "get to the bottom of this" can comprehend the communication gulf our esotericism has created. If for no other reason, esotericism will have to yield in order to preserve our institutions; the government's computer programs must become a matter of general public knowledge. It is the responsibility of the computer community to educate the public at large so that our teachers, ministers, philosophers, gurus, and street-corner advocates may share in the shaping of goals for future computer use.

Instead of trying to teach everyone binary arithmetic, we should attempt to make available to the public the great metaphors which have shaped computer development. In that way, people may come to understand printout. A public which takes a more critical view of computer printout may be the kind of incentive our profession needs to start printing out something meaningful. Teleconferencing short-circuits this problem, reducing the computing components to switching networks. This is useful, but one does not wish to short-circuit the digital store; that would be as if the first human to notice a piece of flint chipped so that it had a useful edge had thrown it at a rabbit, missed, and forgotten about the whole thing.

Unfortunately, present computer metaphors are both limited and poorly understood. For example, most nonprogrammers trying to make heads or tails of computer printout either deal with metaphors which aren't really there or reach back to grasp metaphors some unknown programmer was unaware of passing along; in so doing, they often attribute meaning and significance where it simply was not intended. The meaning of printout at present can be grasped accurately only by those to whom the metaphors of the machine do speak and by whom the limitations of the computer are clearly understood.

OUTPUT TAKES ON MEANING AND CONFUSION ENSUES

When speaking face to face with someone, one perceives many hints as to the reliability of the information one is receiving. In written communication this is more subtle but still very real; we discount what we read in paper X more than what we read in paper Y, we tend to value reports from assistant A more than reports from assistant B, and so on. Reliability here depends in large part on considerations independent of the channel, but in the case of computers, unless you know how they work, you probably have no independent information about reliability.

I. A. Richards tells us: "A sentence we speak or write—like any other line of behavior—will realize some possibilities and fail to realize others."[10] The same is clearly true of a sentence we output, but few programmers seem to look at it that way. For example, imagine a programmer who has a fixed number of bytes available for comments on student report cards. The programmer goes around rather lightheartedly soliciting opinions and suggestions about what might be good comments to put in the system. Little thought is given to the thousands (or millions, if the code is good; good code tends to last) of parents who will pore over these comments trying to learn something about their children. For guessing "*what* makes *what* seem to mean *what—when, where*, and to *whom*" (I. A. Richards),[11] the Equity Funding programmers, though larcenous, were outstanding in their field.

It is important to emphasize that a sentence, even if transmitted without gestures or intonation, is perceived as a broad-band communication, not the simple denoter or token that most programmers know their output to be. Richards says that an utterance may perform any or all of the following sorts of work: indicating, characterizing, realizing, valuing, influencing, controlling, and purposing.[12] The programmer with a fixed number of bytes for precoded comments should be pondering the ponderous communication task placed on his or her shoulders: facilitating the transmission of meaningful information from teacher to student and parent rather than concentrating on puzzle solving.

When this program is in production, a typical report card might look like this:

Reading	A	
Writing	B+	
Arithmetic	C	Comments: DOES NOT WORK UP TO POTENTIAL
Gym	A	
Music	B−	
Shop	A−	

Imagine a typical father examining this report on his child. The father quickly skims over the grades, which seem pretty good and fairly straightforward, and proceeds to try to extract some information from that cryptic comment. He perceives the comment as a message about his child from the child's teacher. Chances are, the father doesn't even realize that the teacher only has a fixed list of canned remarks from which to choose. In fact, simply knowing the comments not chosen would convey more information.

Following Richards's analysis, the father will try to determine what the comment points to ('' my child's character''), what it says about what it points to (''defective''), what it awakens (''I have failed, my child has failed''), what value is imparted (''bad''), what change is indicated (''my child must work harder''), what direction to take (''no more television on weeknights, by God''), what is the purpose (''working up to potential is next to cleanliness''), and finally, after all that stewing, a little calm reflection and venting (''I wonder why that teacher has it in for my kid? Probably sore because plumbers make more money.'').

This also shows how important context can be. The same person who will worry about a trivial comment on a computerized report card is by now knowledgeable enough to ignore the most sophisticated junk mail:

> DEAR BOB: FOR A LIMITED TIME ONLY A SELECT NUMBER OF PLUMBERS ON WILLOWBY STREET HAVE A RARE INVESTMENT OPPORTUNITY IN ARIZONA LAND. . . .

''BUT THE KING OF ENGLAND MAY NOT ENTER''— WILLIAM PITT, THE YOUNGER

The most serious abuse of computer systems so far is the threat to personal privacy. There are still people who miss the point about the common complaint that we are all being turned into numbers; they seem to think the problem is trying to remember one's number. This is called the Benign Presumption. The problem is having a number, not remembering it, because having a number makes collection of information about one person from a number of files an easy task for the computer.

Such file building goes against a deeply held and characteristically American conviction—the belief that every person's background and past is private, that every person should have the right to make a new life, and that self-fulfillment is most likely in an environment with minimum constraints. Americans across the political spectrum hold this view firmly, and yet the march of events is precisely in the opposite direction, led by numerous government agencies and retail credit bureaus. How did such a state of affairs come about? Ignorance, for one thing. But a greater force, we feel, is the tendency for humans to adapt to computers rather than vice versa. Part of the blame falls on programming because current programming is not adaptable.

A news item appearing in the *Des Moines Register* commented: "Compounding the risk is the permanent storage, rapid retrieval and national coverage of a computer-based criminal justice information system that will never suffer from apathy, charity or a bad memory."[13] It is a mistake for anyone to imagine that he or she is so pure as never to be at risk from such a system. We are all vulnerable, and isn't it an affront to our profession to imply that we cannot make storage charitable? Surely we have progressed beyond the stage where value judgments must be designed into the data structure. They should be moved to input parameters.

The fact that computers make keeping dossiers on citizens cheaper is the heart of the privacy problem; the fact that they make the calculation of the pseudofeasibility of any new proposal cheaper contributes to instability and adds to the too-much problem. If one sees the computer as a threat to privacy and stability, the threat is essentially economic; i.e., snooping is now cheaper. Few people would be willing to bite the bullet for a nonprivate unstable world, although many would ally themselves with progress and deprecate the new Luddites. The trouble with "cheaper" is that it seems to get beyond the control of programmers, architects, and engineers. They design better, and cheaper invasion of privacy crops up as a sort of unwanted by-product.

THUMBS DOWN

The potential for instability of so-called "instant democracy" should be considered before the technology completely alters our lives in an undesirable direction. The idea of a terminal of some sort in every home, on which the voter could instantly express pleasure or displeasure on every issue, seems to some like the ultimate in true democracy. From another point of view, it could easily deteriorate into something very much like mob rule. Not enough is known as yet about the decision-making process or how consensus is arrived at and expressed in the election of some candidates over others to justify short-circuiting the representative character of our method of government.

Congress is frequently criticized for being slow and cumbersome. On the other hand, it can be argued that a measured approach is more likely to be thoughtful and intelligent; and because feedback loops that are too short generate instability, a radically shortened feedback loop in the democratic process may produce very undesirable effects. Clearly, this is an area in which serious thought must be given to the consequences of change rather than simply letting change be dictated by technological availability.

ORGANIC COMPUTING

Descriptions of information society sometimes seem to have more to do with what is wrong with Industrial Society than what will be right about Information Society as its successor. Because we seem to be using up resources at an alarming rate, and in the process polluting our surroundings with noise, confusion, and harmful chemicals, it seems clear that changes in our life-style are inevitable. One possibility, for the industrialized societies at least, is a change of emphasis from consumption to what the Japanese call "self-actualization."

There is already the beginning of a trend in this direction, represented by renewed interest in the simpler things of life; protecting our natural surroundings; repairing, reusing, and recycling; preserving the old forms of music, art, and family relationships; and cherishing our ethnic diversity. Still, in our world at least, one can only go forward, and so technology is here to stay and we must learn to live with and love it.

Lynn White has pointed out that "technology does not dictate the shape of human life" but rather "is itself shaped by the dominant values of society."[14] Thus, it is to the revision of our values that we must first attend. We need to see the universe as a whole and ourselves as part of that whole, as the Zen Buddhists do and as Fuller has tried to teach us. For too long, Western humanity has regarded the earth and its nonhuman inhabitants and human-made artifacts as things apart from ourselves to be mastered and exploited. Seeing it all instead as a whole system which includes humans, technology, and "nature"—a system which can be livable only if kept in balance—will help us put our situation in a better perspective.

Computers represent a dangerous new technology, but all our technologies have been dangerous; change of any sort, though inevitable, invariably causes dislocations, pain, and worse. We do not minimize the dangers; they are very real and must be dealt with. We don't believe that those dangers will be met by silencing, ignoring, or steamrolling the critics, as business people with their eyes too closely focused on profits are sometimes inclined to do. On the other hand, we don't believe that those dangers will be adequately met by stamping out business people or machines.

What we are suggesting is that we see our machines as a part of that organic whole which includes all of us and all of them (whoever your particular "them" may be): fishes and factories, rocks and rivers, culture and counterculture. Business people's children will need clean air and water and respect for their privacy; the children of the antitechnologists will need computers to help them navigate space and send back news to the folks at home. Programmers' children will want to see their parents as architects of new ways of life.

A recent national survey (conducted by Louis Harris and Associates, Inc.) reveals that although 54 percent of Americans see computers as a threat to personal privacy (an increase of 17 percent since 1976), 60 percent of those polled believe computers have improved the quality of life in this country.[15] These findings indicate that despite some negative attitudes toward computers, the possibility exists for building well-informed public support for professional, technological, and business goals that are in the best interest of both the industry and the public. The responsibility for developing these goals belongs equally to the programming profession and to the industry at large. Leadership in any sector of society carries with it obligations beyond the immediate boundaries of that sector. Programmers must come to recognize that their work falls into the transmit whether they want it there or not.

Programming may someday be, as Von Neumann suggested, the true queen of the sciences. Programmers, like the members of any profession, bear a special responsibility to their fellow human beings. We have suggested that technology embodies the functions of explorer/scout. Think of the scouts in the old cavalry movies: They didn't have to wear uniforms; they rode out, looked around, and then came back to lead. The cavalry needed the scout, but equally as important and less often recognized, the scout needed the cavalry. It was to their ends he scouted, and it was in terms of their known properties that a plan had to be designed. The plan had to have new insights based on acquisitive, adaptive, active scouting and known goals and constraints.

We must get the information channels of programming itself into manageable shape and think a little about the past (where we've been) and a lot about the future (where we're going). When information society is ushered in with all its opportunities, will programmers stay locked in their cubicles or will they step out to become world citizens?

REFERENCES

CHAPTER ONE

1. Albert Szent-Györgyi, *The Living State and Cancer,* New York, Marcel Dekker, 1978, p. 2.
2. Hugh Kenner, *Bucky: A Guided Tour of Buckminster Fuller,* New York, William Morrow, 1973, pp. 6–8.
3. Ibid., p. 6.
4. Ibid., p. 63.
5. Stephen Toulmin, *Human Understanding,* vol. 1, Princeton, Princeton University Press, 1972, p. 364.
6. Ibid., p. 379.
7. Ibid., p. 366.
8. Ibid., p. 369.
9. Ibid., p. 398.

CHAPTER TWO

1. Stephen Toulmin, *Human Understanding,* vol. 1, Princeton, Princeton University Press, 1972, p. 158.
2. Japan Computer Usage Development Institute Computerization Committee, "The Plan for Information Society—A National Goal toward Year 2000," Final Report, May 1972.
3. Hugh Kenner, *Bucky: A Guided Tour of Buckminster Fuller,* New York, William Morrow, 1973, p. 53.

4. Ibid., pp. 60–63

5. Ibid., p. 124.

6. Arthur W. J. G. Ord-Hume, *Clockwork Music: An Illustrated History of Mechanical Musical Instruments from the Musical Box to the Pianola, from Automaton Lady Virginal Players to Orchestrion*, London, George Allen & Unwin, 1973, p. 18.

7. Lynn White, Jr., *Medieval Technology and Social Change*, London, Oxford University Press, 1964, p. 122.

8. Ibid., p. 124.

9. Lewis Mumford, *Technics and Civilization*, New York, Harcourt Brace Jovanovich, 1934, pp. 14, 15.

10. Arnold Dolmetsch, *The Interpretation of the Music of the XVII and XVIII Centuries: Revealed by Contemporary Evidence*, London, Oxford University Press, 1946, p. 1.

11. Alexander Buckner, *Mechanical Musical Instruments*, Iris Unwin (trans.), London, Batchworth Press, 1959, p. 59.

12. Larry Givens, *Re-enacting the Artist: A Story of the Ampico Reproducing Piano*, Vestal, N. Y., Vestal Press, 1970, p. 8.

CHAPTER THREE

1. Robert J. Braidwood, *Prehistoric Men*, 7th ed., Glenview, Ill., Scott, Foresman, 1967, p. 72.

2. Ronald Stamper, *Information in Business and Administrative Systems*, London, B. T. Batsford, 1973, p. 272.

3. Braidwood, op cit., p. 75.

4. Willis W. Ware, "The Ultimate Computer," *IEEE Spectrum*, vol. 9, no. 3, March 1972, pp. 84–91. For a more recent confirmation of this estimate, see Willis Ware, "Computers and Personal Privacy," *Proceedings of the American Philosophical Society*, vol. 121, no. 5, October 1977, p. 355.

5. Hugh Kenner, *Bucky: A Guided Tour of Buckminster Fuller*, New York, William Morrow, 1973, p. 63.

6. Ibid., p. 128.

7. Ibid., pp. 21, 22.

8. Ibid., p. 39.

9. Ibid., p. 43.
10. Ibid., p. 63.
11. Ibid.
12. Braidwood, op cit., p. 88.
13. Japan Computer Usage Development Institute Computerization Committee, "The Plan for Information Society—A National Goal toward Year 2000," Final Report, May 1972.

CHAPTER FOUR

1. For a description of Von Kempelen's Chess Player, see Arthur W. J. G. Ord-Hume, *Clockwork Music: An Illustrated History of Mechanical Musical Instruments from the Musical Box to the Pianola, from Automaton Lady Virginal Players to Orchestrion,* London, George Allen & Unwin, 1973, pp. 56–59.
2. Hubert L. Dreyfus, "Alchemy and Artificial Intelligence," Santa Monica, Cal., Rand Corporation Paper P-3244, 1965 machine copy.
3. Ibid., p. 13.
4. Cora A. Sowa and John F. Sowa, "Thought Clusters in Early Greek Oral Poetry," *Computers and the Humanities,* vol. 8, 1974, pp. 131–146.
5. Ibid., p. 131.
6. Ibid., p. 137.
7. Ibid., p. 136.
8. Ibid., p. 138.
9. Ibid., p. 145.
10. Ibid.
11. Stephen Toulmin, "The Importance of Norbert Wiener," in Zenon W. Pylyshyn (ed.), *Perspectives on the Computer Revolution,* Englewood Cliffs, N. J., Prentice-Hall, 1970, pp. 147–154.

CHAPTER FIVE

1. Paul Ziff, *Understanding Understanding,* Ithaca, N. Y., Cornell University Press, 1972, pp. 76, 77.
2. John G. Kemeny, *Man and the Computer,* New York, Scribner's, 1972, p. 108.

3. Ronald Stamper, *Information in Business and Administration Systems,* London, B. T. Batsford, 1973, p. 71.
4. Ibid., p. 73.
5. Hubert Dreyfus, *What Computers Can't Do: The Limits of Artificial Intelligence,* rev. ed., New York, Harper & Row, 1979, p. 235.
6. *Computerworld,* vol. 7, 23 May 1973, p. 21.
7. Pieter Dullemeijer, "Some Methodology Problems in a Holistic Approach to Functional Morphology," *Acta Biotheoretica,* vol. 18, 1968, pp. 203–214; and Pieter Dullemeijer, "Craniofacial Biology: A Zoologist's View," *American Journal of Orthodontics,* vol. 59, 1971, pp. 19–23.
8. George J. Klir, "Preview: The Polyphonic General Systems Theory," in George J. Klir (ed.), *Trends in General Systems Theory,* New York, Wiley/Interscience, 1972, p. 1.
9. Ibid.
10. Ibid., p. 3.
11. Gerald M. Weinberg, "A Computer Approach to General Systems Theory," in *Trends,* p. 102.
12. Ibid., p. 104.
13. Ibid.
14. Francis M. Sibley, "How to Read I. A. Richards," *American Scholar,* Spring 1973, pp. 318–378.

CHAPTER SIX

1. Hugh Kenner, *Bucky: A Guided Tour of Buckminster Fuller,* New York, William Morrow, 1973, p. 319.
2. Anatol Rapoport, "The Uses of Mathematical Isomorphism in General Systems Theory," in George J. Klir (ed.), *Trends in General Systems Theory,* New York, Wiley-Interscience, 1972, p. 45.
3. A. A. Yurko, "The Origins of the Information Crisis: Toward a Statement of the Problem," *Automatic Documentation and Mathematical Linguistics,* vol. 5, no. 2, 1971, p. 3.
4. Gerald M. Weinberg, "A Computer Approach to General Systems Theory," in *Trends,* p. 115.
5. Ibid., p. 122.

6. Hubert Dreyfus, "The Critique of Artificial Reason," in Marjorie Grene (ed.), *Interpretations of Life and Mind: Essays around the Problem of Reduction*, London, Routledge & Kegan Paul, 1971, p. 105.

7. Ibid., p. 107.

8. Ibid., p. 106.

9. A. M. Turing, "On Computable Numbers with an Application of the *Entscheidungsproblem*," *Proceedings of the London Mathematical Society*, vol. 42, no. 2, 1937, pp. 230–265. Kurt Gödel, *On Formally Undecidable Propositions of Principia Mathematica and Related Systems*, B. Meltzer (trans.), New York, Basic Books, 1962.

10. I. A. Richards, *Speculative Instruments*, Chicago, University of Chicago Press, 1955, p. 41.

11. Ibid., p. 43.

12. Ibid., p. 48.

13. Wilbur and Orville Wright, *The Papers of Wilbur and Orville Wright: Including the Chanute-Wright Letters and Other Papers of Octave Chanute*, vol. 1, *1899–1905*, Marvin W. McFarland (ed.), New York, McGraw-Hill, 1953, pp. 15, 16.

14. For a complete discussion of these issues, see Hubert L. Dreyfus, *What Computers Can't Do: The Limits of Artificial Intelligence*, rev. ed., New York, Harper & Row, 1979.

15. Stephen Toulmin, *Human Understanding*, vol. 1, Princeton, Princeton University Press, 1972, p. 427.

16. Ibid.

17. Gerald M. Weinberg, *The Psychology of Computer Programming*, New York, D. Van Nostrand, 1971, p. 214.

18. Ronald Stamper, *Information in Business and Administrative Systems*, London, B. T. Batsford, 1973, pp. 38, 39.

CHAPTER SEVEN

1. A. A. Yurko, "The Origins of the Information Crisis: Toward a Statement of the Problem," *Automatic Documentation and Mathematical Linguistics*, vol. 5, no. 2, 1971, pp. 1–5.

2. Ibid., p. 4.

3. Ibid.

4. Martha E. Williams, "Database and Online Statistics—1977," *Bulletin of the American Society for Information Science*, vol. 4, no. 2, December 1977, pp. 21–23.
5. For a detailed description of available on-line systems, see J. L. Hall, *On-line Informational Retrieval Sourcebook*, London, Aslib, 1977.
6. Donald T. Hawkins and Betty Miller, "On-line Database Coverage of the On-line Information Retrieval Literature," *On-line Review*, vol. 1, no. 1, 1977, pp. 59–64.
7. For the most complete study to date of institutional user response to on-line searching, see Judith Wanger, Carlos A. Cuadra, and Mary Fishburn, *Impact of On-line Retrieval Services: A Survey of Users, 1974–1975*, Santa Monica, Cal., Systems Development Corporation, 1976.
8. G. Voiskunskii and V. I. Frants, "Automatic Operational Feedback in a Descriptor IRS," *Automatic Documentation and Mathematical Linguistics*, vol. 5, no. 3, 1971, pp. 28–31.
9. David Pager, "A Proposal for a Computer-based Interactive Scientific Community," *Communications of the ACM*, vol. 15, no. 2, 1972, pp. 71–75.
10. Ibid., p. 74.
11. Donald F. Calhoun, "Hardware Technology," in Alfonso F. Cardenas, Leon Presser, and Miquel A. Marin (eds.), *Computer Science*, New York, Wiley-Interscience, 1972, p. 30.
12. Lucian J. Endicott, Jr., and Peter H. Huyck, "De Ludi Natura Liber Secundus," *Datamation*, Dec. 1, 1971, pp. 32–36. Many of the ideas in this book were first discussed in this and the following two articles: Lucian J. Endicott, Jr., and Peter H. Huyck, "De Ludi Natura," *Datamation*, Feb. 1, 1971, pp. 34–36; and Peter H. Huyck, "CAI Techniques for Information Retrieval," *Datamation*, Feb. 1973, pp. 91–92.
13. Gerald M. Weinberg, *The Psychology of Computer Programming*, New York, D. Van Nostrand, 1971, p. 237.
14. Lewis M. Branscomb, "Information: The Ultimate Frontier," *Science*, vol. 203, Jan. 12, 1978, pp. 143–147.

CHAPTER EIGHT

1. Japan Computer Usage Development Institute Computerization Committee, "The Plan for Information Society—A National Goal toward Year 2000," Final Report, May 1972.

2. For one view of what computer networking might be and a discussion of potential problems, see Starr R. Hiltz and Murray Turoff, *The Network Nation: Human Communication via Computer,* Reading, Mass., Addison-Wesley, 1978.

3. For a discussion of the issues surrounding such regulation, see Anthony G. Oettinger, Paul J. Berman, and William H. Read, *High and Low Politics: Information Resources for the 80s,* Cambridge, Mass., Ballinger, 1977.

4. Jonathan Benthall, *Science and Technology Today,* New York, Praeger, 1972, p. 19.

5. Japan Computer Usage Development Institute Computerization Committee, op. cit.

6. Ibid., p. 1.

7. Ibid., p. 2.

8. Personal communication, June 1979, Yoneji Masuda, President, Institute for Information Society, Fujimura Bldg. 2-15-29, Shinjuko Shinjukuko, Tokyo, Japan.

9. Japan Computer Usage Development Institute Computerization Committee, op cit., p. 4.

10. I. A. Richards, *Speculative Instruments,* Chicago, University of Chicago Press, 1955, p. 5.

11. Ibid., p. 26.

12. Ibid., p. 18.

13. *Des Moines Register,* Nov. 5, 1973, p. 13.

14. Lynn White, "Study of Medieval Technology 1924–1974," *Technology and Culture,* vol. 16, no. 4, 1975, pp. 519–530.

15. Jake Kirchner, "Panel Cites Snowballing Fear of DP," *Computerworld,* June 11, 1979, p. 1; and Marguerite Harris," Harris Poll," *Computerworld,* June 11, 1979, p. 35.

INDEX

INDEX